EMPLOYMENT DISCRIMINATION LAW UNDER TITLE VII

Second Edition

by

Margaret C. Jasper

Legal Almanac Series:
Thomson Reuters' Law for the Layperson

WEST®
A Thomson Reuters business

For Customer Assistance Call 1-800-328-4880

Mat #41218326

ISBN # 978-0-314-60520-7

To My Husband Chris

Your love and support

are my motivation and inspiration

To My Sons, Michael, Nick and Chris

-and-

In memory of my son, Jimmy

Table of Contents

CHAPTER 2:
FILING A DISCRIMINATION CHARGE

CHAPTER 3: THE EEOC MEDIATION PROGRAM

CHAPTER 4: DISCRIMINATION ON THE BASIS OF RACE OR COLOR

CHAPTER 5: DISCRIMINATION ON THE BASIS OF RELIGION

CHAPTER 6:
DISCRIMINATION ON THE BASIS OF SEX

CHAPTER 7:
DISCRIMINATION ON THE BASIS OF NATIONAL ORIGIN

CHAPTER 8:
DISCRIMINATION ON THE BASIS OF AGE

CHAPTER 9:
DISCRIMINATION ON THE BASIS OF DISABILITY

CHAPTER 10: ADDITIONAL BASIS OF DISCRIMINATION

APPENDICES

ABOUT THE AUTHOR

MARGARET C. JASPER is an attorney engaged in the general practice of law in South Salem, New York, concentrating in the areas of personal injury and entertainment law. Ms. Jasper holds a Juris Doctor degree from Pace University School of Law, White Plains, New York, is a member of the New York and Connecticut bars, and is certified to practice before the United States District Courts for the Southern and Eastern Districts of New York, the United States Court of Appeals for the Second Circuit, and the United States Supreme Court.

Ms. Jasper has been appointed to the law guardian panel for the Family Court of the State of New York, is a member of a number of professional organizations and associations, and is a New York State licensed real estate broker operating as Jasper Real Estate, in South Salem, New York.

Margaret Jasper maintains a website at http://www.JasperLaw Office.com.

In 2004, Ms. Jasper successfully argued a case before the New York Court of Appeals, which gives mothers of babies who are stillborn due to medical negligence the right to bring a legal action and recover emotional distress damages. This successful appeal overturned a 26-year old New York case precedent, which previously prevented mothers of stillborn babies from suing their negligent medical providers.

Ms. Jasper is the author and general editor of the following legal Almanacs:

Adoption Law

AIDS Law

The Americans with Disabilities Act

Animal Rights Law

Auto Leasing

Bankruptcy Law for the Individual Debtor

Banks and their Customers

Becoming a Citizen

Buying and Selling Your Home

Commercial Law

Consumer Rights and the Law

Co-ops and Condominiums: Your Rights and Obligations As Owner

Copyright Law

Credit Cards and the Law

Custodial Rights

Dealing with Debt

Dictionary of Selected Legal Terms

Drunk Driving Law

DWI, DUI and the Law

Education Law

Elder Law

Employee Rights in the Workplace

Employment Discrimination Under Title VII

Environmental Law

Estate Planning

Everyday Legal Forms

Executors and Personal Representatives: Rights and Responsibilities

Guardianship and the Law

Harassment in the Workplace

Health Care and Your Rights

Health Care Directives

Hiring Household Help and Contractors: Your Rights and Obligations Under the Law

Home Mortgage Law Primer

Hospital Liability Law

How To Change Your Name

How To Form an LLC

How To Protect Your Challenged Child

How To Start Your Own Business

Identity Theft and How To Protect Yourself

Individual Bankruptcy and Restructuring

Injured on the Job: Employee Rights, Worker's Compensation and Disability Insurance Law

International Adoption

Juvenile Justice and Children's Law

Labor Law

Landlord-Tenant Law

Law for the Small Business Owner

The Law of Attachment and Garnishment

The Law of Buying and Selling

The Law of Capital Punishment

The Law of Child Custody

The Law of Contracts

The Law of Debt Collection

The Law of Dispute Resolution

The Law of Immigration

The Law of Libel and Slander

The Law of Medical Malpractice

The Law of No-Fault Insurance

The Law of Obscenity and Pornography

The Law of Personal Injury

The Law of Premises Liability

The Law of Product Liability

The Law of Speech and the First Amendment

Lemon Laws

Living Together: Practical Legal Issues

Marriage and Divorce

Missing and Exploited Children: How to Protect Your Child
Motor Vehicle Law
Nursing Home Negligence
Patent Law
Pet Law
Prescription Drugs
Privacy and the Internet: Your Rights and Expectations Under the Law
Probate Law
Protecting Your Business: Disaster Preparation and the Law
Real Estate Law for the Homeowner and Broker
Religion and the Law
Retirement Planning
The Right to Die
Rights of Single Parents
Small Claims Court
Social Security Law
Special Education Law
Teenagers and Substance Abuse
Trademark Law
Trouble Next Door: What to do With Your Neighbor
Victim's Rights Law
Violence Against Women
Welfare: Your Rights and the Law
What if It Happened to You: Violent Crimes and Victims' Rights
What if the Product Doesn't Work: Warranties & Guarantees
Workers' Compensation Law
Your Child's Legal Rights: An Overview
Your Rights in a Class Action Suit
Your Rights as a Tenant
Your Rights Under the Family and Medical Leave Act
You've Been Fired: Your Rights and Remedies

INTRODUCTION

Employment discrimination refers to the illegal practice of making employment decisions based on an employee's age, race, sex, religion, national origin, or physical disability. The primary federal anti-discrimination statute is Title VII of the Civil Rights Act of 1964, as amended, with which this Almanac is concerned. The United States Equal Employment Opportunity Commission (EEOC) was established by Title VII, and is responsible for interpreting and enforcing the provisions of the Act.

As more fully discussed in this Almanac, Title VII prohibits discrimination in hiring, promotion, discharge, pay, fringe benefits, and other aspects of employment, on the basis of race, color, religion, sex, or national origin. Most private employers, state and local governments, educational institutions, employment agencies, and labor organizations are subject to Title VII, which covers both current employees and job applicants.

There are also a number of other federal and state statutes which prohibit employment discrimination. The Americans with Disabilities Act of 1990 prohibits employment discrimination against individuals with disabilities. The Age Discrimination in Employment Act of 1967 prohibits discrimination against individuals because of their age.

Some of the state laws are patterned after the federal statutes, and provide similar protection to workers employed by those employers not covered under the federal statutes. Some state laws also extend protection to additional groups not covered by the federal laws. Thus, the reader is advised to check the laws of his or her own jurisdiction when researching employment discrimination matters.

The Appendices provide resource directories, relevant statutes, and other pertinent information and data. The Glossary contains definitions of many of the terms used throughout the Almanac.

CHAPTER 1: OVERVIEW OF DISCRIMINATION IN THE WORKPLACE

HISTORY OF EMPLOYMENT DISCRIMINATION LAW

The prohibitions of employment discrimination set forth in Title VII had their roots in the Unemployment Relief Act of 1933, which provided "[t]hat in employing citizens for the purpose of this Act no discrimination shall be made on account of race, color, or creed."

The administrations of Presidents Roosevelt, Truman, Eisenhower, and Kennedy all created Fair Employment Practices Committees to investigate complaints of discrimination against businesses with federal contracts. Legislation proposed by President Kennedy in 1963 simply continued the long-standing practice of attempting to eradicate discrimination by those doing business with the federal government through voluntary compliance, without any enforcement mechanisms.

The 1963 amendments to the Civil Rights Bill broadened the scope of anti-discrimination legislation by: (1) making it applicable to all employers with more than 25 employees; and (2) creating the Equal Employment Opportunity Commission (EEOC), which became the enforcement agency for the federal anti-discrimination statutes.

Passage of Title VII

In 1964, Title VII of the Civil Rights Act was passed and signed into law by President Johnson. Title VII, as enacted, prohibited discrimination in employment decisions because of an individual's "race, color, religion, sex, or national origin." Title VII further prohibited "limiting, segregating, or classifying employees or applicants in any way that would deprive them of employment opportunities or adversely affect their status because of their race, color, religion, sex, or national origin."

Following its enactment, thousands of people began to file charges with the newly created EEOC.

Inclusion of the Sex Amendment

Although the Civil Rights Act was enacted primarily in response to demands for racial justice and equality, from its inception it also prohibited discrimination on the basis of religion, sex, and national origin. The proposal to include sex originated with the National Women's Party, which had been lobbying for the Equal Rights Amendment since 1923, and which had sought to include sex in every civil rights bill considered by Congress for forty years. However, the inclusion of sex as a prohibited basis in Title VII is believed to have been an attempt by a southern opponent of civil rights legislation to actually derail the legislation by including the "sex amendment." This tactic was unsuccessful and the legislation passed.

The unexpected inclusion of sex in the statute quickly led women workers and the newly emerging women's movement of the late 1960s to take advantage of the opportunity to pursue equality in the courts. In the first year after enactment, one-third of the charges filed with the EEOC alleged sex discrimination.

Strengthening the Remedies

In the late 1980s and early 1990s, civil rights activists expressed their frustration with the inability of the existing remedies available under Title VII to adequately compensate victims and deter discrimination. These inadequacies were subsequently addressed by passage of the Civil Rights Act of 1991, which added compensatory and punitive damages to the remedies available to victims of intentional discrimination. As a result, Title VII cases also became eligible for trial by jury because the Seventh Amendment mandates the availability of jury trials whenever damages may be awarded.

WHAT IS EMPLOYMENT DISCRIMINATION?

Unless there is an employment agreement for a certain term, in most states, an employer can discharge or lay off any of its employees, with or without cause, and with or without notice, even when the discharge is unfair or unreasonable. In turn, an employee is entitled to quit their job without repercussion, absent an employment agreement. This is known as "employment at will"—a common law doctrine that basically says your employer can't force you to stay, and you can't force the employer to keep you on as an employee.

Although the employment at will doctrine states that either party may end the employment relationship without prior notice, an employee cannot be discharged in violation of federal or state anti-discrimination laws, as further discussed below. If you are discharged and you suspect that your dismissal was in violation of an anti-discrimination law, you should examine the circumstances surrounding your dismissal to determine whether your discharge was, in fact, the result of unlawful employment discrimination.

Employment discrimination refers to the illegal practice of making employment decisions, such as termination of employment, based on an employee's age, race, sex, religion, national origin, or physical disability. In addition, some jurisdictions also prohibit employers from discharging employees on account of their marital status, political affiliation, and sexual orientation.

Employment discrimination may occur in three situations:

1. An employer treats similar employees differently.
2. An employer's actions against an employee are based on prejudice.
3. An employment decision seems fair, but it actually has a negative effect on a group of employees in a protected class.

The first two types of discrimination are pretty clear. The third type may take some analysis to understand the discriminatory action.

For example, if an employer lays off all employees who do not have college degrees, this may appear to be fair because the layoff affects a specific group of employees who are similarly situated. However, if most of the employees who do not have college degrees are women, and almost all of the employees who have college degrees are men, the layoff would have an "adverse impact" on women employees. Insofar as gender is a protected class under Title VII, the layoff could be deemed illegal.

Many state laws are patterned after the federal statutes, and provide similar protection to workers employed by those employers not covered under the federal statutes. Some state laws also extend protection to additional groups not covered by the federal laws. Thus, the reader is advised to check the laws of his or her own jurisdiction when researching employment discrimination matters.

EMPLOYMENT DISCRIMINATION UNDER TITLE VII

Title VII of the Civil Rights Act of 1964 prohibits discrimination in employment against individuals because of their race, color, national origin, religion or sex. Title VII prohibits not only intentional discrimination, but also practices that have the "effect" of discriminating against individuals on these bases. As discussed below, the U.S. Equal Employment Opportunity Commission (EEOC) enforces all of these laws.

Covered Employers

Title VII covers all private employers, state and local governments, and education institutions that employ 15 or more individuals. These laws also cover private and public employment agencies, labor organizations, and joint labor management committees controlling apprenticeship and training.

Title VII also covers the federal government. However, as more fully discussed in Chapter 2, "Filing a Discrimination Charge," there are different procedures used for processing complaints of federal employment discrimination.

Prohibited Actions

Terms of Employment

Under Title VII, it is illegal to discriminate in any aspect of employment, including:

1. Hiring and firing;
2. Compensation, assignment, or classification of employees;
3. Transfer, promotion, layoff, or recall;
4. Job advertisements;
5. Recruitment;
6. Testing;
7. Use of company facilities;
8. Training and apprenticeship programs;
9. Fringe benefits;
10. Pay, retirement plans, and disability leave; or
11. Other terms and conditions of employment.

Harassment

Harassing an individual on the basis of race, color, religion, sex or national origin is prohibited under Title VII.

Retaliation

As discussed below, retaliation against an individual for: (1) filing a charge of discrimination, (2) participating in an EEOC investigation, or (3) opposing discriminatory practices, is prohibited under Title VII.

Stereotyping

Employment decisions based on stereotypes or assumptions about the abilities, traits, or performance of individuals of a certain sex, race, religion, or ethnic group are prohibited under Title VII.

Association with Covered Individual

Denying employment opportunities to a person because of marriage to, or association with, an individual of a particular race, religion, or national origin is prohibited under Title VII. In addition, discrimination because of an individual's participation in schools or places of worship associated with a particular racial, ethnic, or religious group is prohibited.

RETALIATION

An employer may not fire an individual for filing a charge of discrimination, participating in a discrimination proceeding, or otherwise opposing discrimination. The same laws that prohibit discrimination based on race, color, sex, religion, national origin, age, and disability, also prohibit retaliation against individuals who oppose unlawful discrimination or participate in an employment discrimination proceeding.

Retaliation occurs when an employer, employment agency, or labor organization takes an adverse action against a covered individual because he or she engaged in a protected activity. An adverse action—e.g. termination—is an action taken to try to keep someone from opposing a discriminatory practice, or from participating in an employment discrimination proceeding.

Covered Employees

Individuals are covered under the law if they have opposed unlawful practices, participated in proceedings, or requested accommodations related to employment discrimination based on race, color, sex, religion, national origin, age, or disability. Individuals who have a close association with someone who has engaged in such protected activity are also covered individuals. For example, it is illegal to terminate an employee because his spouse participated in employment discrimination litigation.

Protected Activities

Opposition

Protected activity includes opposition to a practice believed to be unlawful discrimination. Opposition is informing an employer that you believe that he or she is engaging in prohibited discrimination. Opposition is protected from retaliation as long as it is based on a reasonable, good-faith belief that the complained of practice violates anti-discrimination laws, and the manner of the opposition is reasonable.

Examples of protected opposition include:

1. Complaining to anyone about alleged discrimination against oneself or others;
2. Threatening to file a charge of discrimination;
3. Picketing in opposition to discrimination; and
4. Refusing to obey an order reasonably believed to be discriminatory.

Participation

Protected activity includes participation in an employment discrimination proceeding. Participation is protected even if the proceeding involved claims that ultimately were found to be invalid.

Examples of participation include:

1. Filing a charge of employment discrimination;
2. Cooperating with an internal investigation of alleged discriminatory practices; and
3. Serving as a witness in an EEOC investigation or litigation.

Reasonable Accommodation

Requesting a reasonable accommodation based on religion or disability is also a protected activity under the law.

Retaliation Statistics

1. In fiscal year 2004, the EEOC received 22,740 charges of retaliation discrimination based on all statutes enforced by EEOC.
2. The EEOC resolved 24,751 retaliation charges in fiscal year 2004, more than were filed during the course of the fiscal year.
3. In fiscal year 2004, the EEOC recovered more than $90 million in monetary benefits for charging parties and other aggrieved individuals, not including monetary benefits obtained through litigation.

THE U.S. EQUAL EMPLOYMENT OPPORTUNITY COMMISSION

The United States Equal Employment Opportunity Commission (EEOC) is an independent federal agency established by Congress in 1964 to enforce Title VII of the Civil Rights Act of 1964. The EEOC began operating on July 2, 1965. It is composed of five Commissioners and a General Counsel appointed by the President and confirmed by the Senate. Commissioners are appointed for five-year staggered terms. The General

Counsel's term is four years. The President designates a Chairman and a Vice-Chairman. The Chairman is the chief executive officer. The Commissioners have the authority to establish equal employment policy and to approve litigation. The General Counsel is responsible for conducting litigation.

The EEOC's mission is to promote equal opportunity in employment through administrative and judicial enforcement of these federal civil rights laws, and through broad-based educational outreach and technical assistance programs. The EEOC provides a range of informational materials and assistance to individuals and entities with rights and responsibilities under EEOC-enforced laws. Most materials and assistance are provided to the public at no cost, including posters advising employees of their equal employment opportunity rights, and pamphlets, manuals, fact sheets, and enforcement guidance on laws enforced by the EEOC.

The EEOC is also responsible for promulgating and issuing regulations and other guidance materials to assist in interpreting the laws it enforces, and for administering the federal sector employment discrimination program. The EEOC also provides funding and support to state and local fair employment practices agencies (FEPAs).

A directory of EEOC offices is set forth in Appendix 1.

Statutory Jurisdiction

The EEOC enforces the following principal federal statutes prohibiting employment discrimination:

Title VII of the Civil Rights Act of 1964

Title VII of the Civil Rights Act of 1964, as amended, prohibits employment discrimination on the basis of race, color, religion, sex, or national origin. This Almanac is primarily concerned with employment discrimination under Title VII.

Discrimination on the bases of race and color, religion, sex, and national origin are discussed more fully in Chapters 4 through 7 of this Almanac.

Selected provisions of Title VII of the Civil Rights Act of 1964 are set forth in Appendix 2.

The Civil Rights Act of 1991

The Civil Rights Act of 1991 amends and assists in the enforcement of Title VII. The Civil Rights Act includes provisions for monetary damages in cases of intentional discrimination and clarifies provisions regarding disparate impact actions.

Selected provisions of the Civil Rights Act of 1991 are set forth in Appendix 3.

The Equal Pay Act of 1963

The Equal Pay Act of 1963 (EPA) prohibits discrimination on the basis of gender in compensation for substantially similar work under similar conditions.

The Equal Pay Act of 1963 is discussed more fully in Chapter 6, "Discrimination on the Basis of Sex," of this Almanac.

Selected provisions of the Equal Pay Act of 1963 are set forth in Appendix 4.

The Age Discrimination in Employment Act of 1967

The Age Discrimination in Employment Act of 1967 (ADEA), as amended, prohibits employment discrimination against individuals 40 years of age and older.

The Age Discrimination in Employment Act is discussed more fully in Chapter 8, "Discrimination on the Basis of Age," of this Almanac.

Selected provisions of the Age Discrimination in Employment Act is set forth in Appendix 5.

Title I of the Americans with Disabilities Act of 1990

Title I of the Americans with Disabilities Act of 1990 (ADA) prohibits employment discrimination on the basis of disability in both the public and private sector, excluding the federal government.

Title I of the ADA is discussed more fully in Chapter 9, "Discrimination on the Basis of Disability," of this Almanac.

Selected provisions of Title I of the Americans with Disabilities Act of 1990 is set forth in Appendix 6.

Section 501 of the Rehabilitation Act of 1973

Section 501 of the Rehabilitation Act of 1973, as amended, prohibits employment discrimination against federal employees with disabilities.

Notice Requirement

Employers are required to post notices to all employees advising them of their rights under the laws that the EEOC enforces, and their right to be free from retaliation. Such notices are required to be accessible, as needed, to persons with visual or other disabilities that affect reading.

Contact Information

The EEOC customer service representatives are available to assist individuals in more than 150 languages. You can reach the EEOC as follows:

Headquarters: U.S. Equal Employment Opportunity Commission
1801 L. Street NW
Washington, DC 20507
Tel: 202-663-4900/TTY: 202-663-4494

EEOC customer service representatives are available to answer questions from 8:00AM to 8:00PM EST. There is also a 24 hour automated line with answers to the most frequently asked questions.

Telephone: 1-800-669-4000
TTY: 1-800-669-6820
Email: info@ask.eeoc.gov

ADDITIONAL ANTI-DISCRIMINATION LEGISLATION

Other federal laws, not enforced by EEOC, also prohibit discrimination and reprisal against federal employees and applicants for federal employment. The Civil Service Reform Act of 1978 (CSRA) contains a number of prohibitions, known as prohibited personnel practices, which are designed to promote overall fairness in federal personnel actions.

The CSRA prohibits any employee who has authority to take certain personnel actions from discriminating for or against employees or applicants for employment on the bases of race, color, national origin, religion, sex, age or disability. It also provides that certain personnel actions cannot be based on status or conduct that does not adversely affect employee performance, such as marital status or political affiliation.

The Office of Personnel Management (OPM) has interpreted the prohibition of discrimination based on conduct to include discrimination based on sexual orientation. The CSRA also prohibits reprisal against federal employees or applicants for whistle blowing, or for exercising an appeal, complaint, or grievance right. The CSRA is enforced by both the Office of Special Counsel (OSC) and the Merit Systems Protection Board (MSPB).

MULTINATIONAL EMPLOYERS

Covered Employers

Multinational employers that operate in the United States or its territories—American Samoa, Guam, the Commonwealth of the Northern Mariana Islands, Puerto Rico, and the U.S. Virgin Islands—are subject to EEO laws to the same extent as U.S. employers. An exception exists if the employer is covered by a treaty or other binding international agreement that limits the full applicability of U.S. anti-discrimination laws, such as one that permits the company to prefer its own nationals for certain positions.

Employers that are incorporated or based in the U.S., or are controlled by U.S. companies, and that employ U.S. citizens outside the United States or its territories, are subject to Title VII, the ADEA, and the ADA with respect to those employees. U.S. EEO laws do not apply to non-U.S. citizens outside the U.S. or its territories.

Covered Employees

All employees who work in the United States or its territories for covered employers are protected by the EEO laws, regardless of their citizenship or work authorization status. Employees who work in the U.S. or its territories are protected whether they work for a U.S. or foreign employer.

Employees of Non-U.S. Employers in the United States

The only exception to the rule that employees working in the U.S. are covered by federal EEO laws occurs when the employer is not a U.S. employer and is subject to a treaty or other binding international agreement that permits the company to prefer its own nationals for certain positions.

Non-Citizens Working Outside the United States

Individuals who are not U.S. citizens are not protected by the U.S. EEO laws when employed outside the U.S. or its territories, although they may be covered by another country's EEO laws.

U.S. Citizens Working Outside the United States

U.S. citizens who are employed outside the United States by a U.S. employer, or a foreign company controlled by a U.S. employer, are protected by Title VII, the ADEA, and the ADA.

How to Determine Who is a U.S. Employer

An employer will be considered a U.S. employer if it is incorporated or based in the United States or if it has sufficient connections with the United States. This is an individualized factual determination that will be based on the following relevant factors:

1. The employer's principal place of business, i.e., the primary place where factories, offices, and other facilities are located;

2. The nationality of dominant shareholders and/or those holding voting control; and

3. The nationality and location of management, including the officers and directors of the company.

How to Determine Whether a Company is "Controlled" by a U.S. Employer

Employers operating outside the United States are covered by Title VII, the ADEA, and the ADA only if they are controlled by a U.S. employer. Whether a company is controlled by a U.S. employer is also an individualized determination, which will be based on the following relevant factors:

1. Whether the operations of the employers are interrelated;
2. Whether there is common management;
3. Whether there is centralized control of labor relations; and
4. Whether there is common ownership or financial control.

Foreign Laws Defense

U.S. employers are not required to comply with the requirements of Title VII, the ADEA, or the ADA, if adherence to that requirement would violate a law of the country where the workplace is located. For example, an employer would have a "Foreign Laws Defense" for a mandatory retirement policy if the law of the country in which the company is located requires mandatory retirement.

Nevertheless, a U.S. employer may not transfer an employee to another country in order to disadvantage the employee because of his or her race, color, sex, religion, national origin, age, or disability. For example, an employer may not transfer an older worker to a country with a mandatory retirement age for the purpose of forcing the employee's retirement.

PROTECTING YOUR RIGHTS IN THE WORKPLACE

Most people do not anticipate becoming the victim of employment discrimination at the time they are hired as an employee. Ideally, such a scenario never occurs, however, there are certain things you should do to preserve your rights in the workplace if you ever have to deal with any type of wrongful termination. It is much more difficult to prevail in a lawsuit if there is no documentation to support your grievances.

For example, every employee should make it a practice to keep a personal employment file that documents their entire relationship with their employer. This is generally referred to as keeping a "paper trail." You should not wait until a problem arises in the workplace to start accumulating evidence.

It is advisable to keep a journal to document any unusual or significant events that occur in the workplace, including the basic facts, e.g. date, time, place, statements made, actions taken, and persons present, etc. In addition, all work-related documents, including employee handbooks, performance evaluations, and memorandums, etc., should be kept in your personal employment file and kept at home. These items may come in handy at some point in the future.

REACHING AN INFORMAL RESOLUTION WITH YOUR EMPLOYER

Problems that arise in the workplace do not always have to involve filing a charge with the EEOC. Some problems can be worked out using informal methods. For example, the employee can try and work the problem out directly with the employer by arranging an informal meeting. Most employers would rather avoid having to answer an EEOC discrimination charge or defend a lawsuit if a legitimate grievance is brought to their attention. If the employee is a member of a union, the union representative may attend the meeting to help informally mediate any disputes.

However, in order to adequately prepare for the meeting with your employer, you must be knowledgeable about your legal rights under the laws that prohibit discrimination in the workplace, including the possible sanctions under the law. You should calmly and intelligently set forth the basic facts surrounding the situation, and explain how your rights were violated. This demonstrates to the employer that you are serious about pursuing legal action.

CHAPTER 2: FILING A DISCRIMINATION CHARGE

IN GENERAL

Any individual who believes that his or her employment rights have been violated may file a charge of discrimination with the Equal Employment Opportunity Commission (EEOC). In addition, an individual, organization, or agency may file a charge on behalf of another person in order to protect the aggrieved person's identity. To protect your legal rights, it is always best to contact the EEOC promptly when discrimination is suspected.

A discrimination charge may be filed by mail or in person at the nearest EEOC office. If the complainant requires an accommodation, such as a sign language interpreter, in order to file a charge, the complainant should notify the EEOC and appropriate arrangements will be made.

Federal sector employees or applicants for employment must file under the Federal Sector Equal Employment Opportunity Complaint Process discussed below.

REQUIRED INFORMATION

In order to file a discrimination charge, certain information must be provided, including:

1. The charging party's name, address, and telephone number;
2. The name, address, and telephone number of the respondent employer, employment agency, or union that is alleged to have discriminated, and the number of employees or union members, if known;
3. A short description of the alleged violation; and
4. The date of the alleged violation.

TIME LIMITATIONS

All laws enforced by the EEOC, except the Equal Pay Act (EPA), require that the charging party file the charge with the EEOC before a private lawsuit may be filed in court. In addition, there are strict time limits within which charges must be filed:

1. A charge must be filed with the EEOC within 180 days from the date of the alleged violation, in order to protect the charging party's rights.

2. The 180-day filing deadline is extended to 300 days if the charge is also covered by a state or local anti-discrimination law.

3. For charges alleging discrimination under the Age Discrimination in Employment Act (ADEA), only state laws extend the filing limit to 300 days.

4. These time limits do not apply to claims under the Equal Pay Act, because under the EPA, persons do not have to file a charge with the EEOC first in order to have the right to file a private lawsuit. However, since many EPA claims also raise Title VII sex discrimination issues, it may be advisable to file charges under both laws within the time limits indicated.

FAIR EMPLOYMENT PRACTICES AGENCIES

A jurisdictional question may arise when a discrimination charge violates both a federal anti-discrimination law and a state or local law. Many states and localities have agencies responsible for enforcing their anti-discrimination laws. The EEOC refers to these agencies as "Fair Employment Practices Agencies (FEPAs).

Through the use of work sharing agreements, the EEOC and the FEPA avoids duplication of effort while at the same time ensuring that a charging party's rights are protected under both federal and state law.

If a charge is filed with a FEPA and is also covered by federal law, the FEPA "dual files" the charge with the EEOC to protect federal rights, however, the charge will usually be retained by the FEPA for handling.

On the other hand, if a charge is filed with the EEOC and is also covered by a state or local law, the EEOC "dual files" the charge with the state or local FEPA, but the EEOC ordinarily retains the charge for handling.

PROCESSING THE DISCRIMINATION CHARGE

After a charge of employment discrimination is filed with the EEOC, the employer is notified that the charge has been filed. From this point there are a number of ways a charge may be handled, as follows:

1. A charge may be assigned for priority investigation if the initial facts appear to support a violation of law. When the evidence is less strong, the charge may be assigned for follow up investigation to determine whether it is likely that a violation has occurred.

2. The EEOC can attempt to settle a charge at any stage of the investigation if the charging party and the employer express an interest in doing so. If settlement efforts are not successful, the investigation continues.

3. In investigating a charge, the EEOC may make written requests for information, interview people, review documents and, as needed, visit the facility where the alleged discrimination occurred. When the investigation is complete, the EEOC will discuss the evidence with the charging party or employer, as appropriate.

4. The charge may be selected for the EEOC's mediation program if both the charging party and the employer express an interest and consent to this option. Mediation is offered as an alternative to a lengthy investigation. Participation in the mediation program is confidential and voluntary. If mediation is unsuccessful, the charge is returned for investigation.

5. A charge may be dismissed at any point if, in the agency's best judgment, further investigation will not establish a violation of the law. A charge may be dismissed at the time it is filed, if an initial in-depth interview does not produce evidence to support the claim.

RESOLVING THE DISCRIMINATION CHARGE

If the evidence obtained in an investigation does not establish that discrimination occurred, the charge will be dismissed and the reasons for dismissal will be explained to the charging party. A notice will be issued that gives the charging party 90 days in which to file a private lawsuit.

If the evidence establishes that discrimination has occurred, the employer and the charging party will be informed of this finding in a letter of determination that explains the reasons for the finding. The EEOC will then attempt conciliation with the employer to develop a remedy for the discrimination.

If the case is successfully conciliated, or has already been successfully mediated or settled, neither the EEOC nor the charging party may go to court unless the conciliation, mediation, or settlement agreement is not honored.

If the EEOC is unable to successfully conciliate the case, the agency will decide whether to bring suit in federal court. If the EEOC decides not to sue, it will issue a notice closing the case and giving the charging party 90 days in which to file a lawsuit on his or her own behalf. In cases brought against state or local governments alleging violations of Title VII or the Americans with Disabilities Act (ADA), the Department of Justice handles the actions.

FILING A PRIVATE LAWSUIT

The charging party may file a private lawsuit within 90 days after receiving a "right to sue" notice from the EEOC, as stated above.

Under Title VII and the ADA, the charging party can also request a "right to sue" notice at least 180 days after the charge was first filed with the EEOC, and may then bring suit within 90 days after receiving this notice.

A Notice of Right to Sue (Issued On Request) is set forth in Appendix 7.

Under the ADEA, a suit may be filed at any time 60 days after filing a charge with the EEOC, but not later than 90 days after the EEOC gives notice that it has completed action on the charge.

Under the EPA, a lawsuit must be filed within two years of the discriminatory act. If the violation was willful, the lawsuit must be filed within three years of the discriminatory act.

REMEDIES

The remedies available for employment discrimination, whether caused by intentional acts or by practices that have a discriminatory effect, may include the following:

1. Back pay;
2. Hiring;
3. Promotion;
4. Reinstatement;
5. Front pay;
6. Reasonable accommodation;

7. Attorney's fees;

8. Expert witness fees;

9. Court costs; and

10. Any other action that would make the charging party "whole"—i.e., in the condition he or she would have been if the discrimination had not occurred.

Compensatory and Punitive Damages

Under most EEOC-enforced laws, compensatory and punitive damages also may be available where intentional discrimination is found. Damages may be available to compensate for actual monetary losses, for future monetary losses, and for mental anguish and inconvenience. Punitive damages also may be available if an employer acted with malice or reckless indifference, however, punitive damages are not available against the federal, state or local governments.

In cases concerning reasonable accommodation under the ADA, compensatory or punitive damages may not be awarded to the charging party if an employer can demonstrate that "good faith" efforts were made to provide a reasonable accommodation.

Notice to Employees

An employer may be required to post notices to all employees addressing the violations of a specific charge and advising them of their rights under the laws EEOC enforces and their right to be free from retaliation. Such notices must be accessible, as needed, to persons with visual or other disabilities that affect reading.

Corrective Action

The employer may also be required to take corrective or preventive actions to cure the source of the identified discrimination and minimize the chance of its recurrence, as well as discontinue the specific discriminatory practices involved in the case.

FILING A COMPLAINT WITH A FEDERAL AGENCY

Employees or applicants who believe that they have been discriminated against by a federal agency have the right to file a complaint with that agency. The first step is to contact an EEO Counselor at the agency within 45 days of the discriminatory action. EEO counselors provide information to the aggrieved individual concerning how the federal sector EEO process works, including time frames and appeal procedures. The EEO counselor also attempts to informally resolve the matter.

EEO Counseling

At the initial counseling session, the EEO counselors must advise the individual, in writing, of their rights and responsibilities in the EEO process, including the right to request a hearing before an EEOC administrative judge, or an immediate final decision from the agency following its investigation of the complaint.

The counselor must also inform the individual of their right to proceed directly to court in a lawsuit under the Age Discrimination in Employment Act (ADEA). Further the individual must also be made aware of their duty to mitigate damages, and the fact that only claims raised in pre-complaint counseling may be alleged in a subsequent complaint filed with the agency.

Ordinarily, counseling must be completed within 30 days. If the matter is not resolved in that time period, the counselor must inform the individual in writing of the right to file a discrimination complaint.

This notice—called a "Notice of Final Interview"—must inform the individual that a complaint must be:

1. Filed within 15 days of receipt of the notice;
2. Identify the agency official with whom the complaint must be filed; and
3. Notify the individual of his or her duty to inform the agency if he or she is represented by an attorney.

The 30-day counseling period may be extended for an additional 60 days under the following conditions:

1. Where the individual agrees to such extension in writing; or
2. Where the aggrieved person chooses to participate in an alternative dispute resolution (ADR) procedure, as discussed below.

Alternative Dispute Resolution

Each agency has established its own alternative dispute resolution (ADR) program for both the pre-complaint process and the formal complaint process. 29 C.F.R. Section 1614.102(b)(2). At the initial counseling session, counselors must advise the individual of their right to choose between participating in the EEO counseling or in the agency's ADR program.

If the individual chooses to participate in the agency ADR program, and the matter is not resolved within 90 days of the date the individual contacted the agency's EEO office, a Notice of Final Interview must be issued to the individual giving him or her the right to proceed with a formal complaint.

Filing a Complaint

At the end of counseling, or if ADR is unsuccessful, the individual may then file a complaint with the agency that allegedly discriminated against the individual. The complaint must be filed within 15 days of receipt of the Notice of Final Interview. The EEO counselor must submit a written report to the agency's EEO office concerning the issues discussed and the actions taken during counseling.

The complaint must be a signed statement from the complainant or the complainant's attorney, containing the complainant's or representative's telephone number and address, and must be sufficiently precise to identify the complainant and the agency, and describe generally the action or practice that forms the basis of the complaint.

The agency must acknowledge receipt of the complaint in writing and inform the complainant of the following:

1. The date on which the complaint was filed;
2. The address of the EEOC office where a request for a hearing should be sent;
3. That the complainant has the right to appeal the agency's final action or dismissal of a complaint; and
4. That the agency must investigate the complaint within 180 days of the filing date.

The agency's acknowledgment must also advise the complainant that when a complaint has been amended, the agency must complete the investigation within the earlier of: (1) 180 days after the last amendment to the complaint; or (2) 360 days after the filing of the original complaint. A complainant may request a hearing from an EEOC administrative judge on the consolidated complaints any time after 180 days from the date of the first filed complaint.

Investigation

The agency must conduct an investigation of the complaint, unless the complaint is dismissed. Investigations are conducted by the respondent agency. The agency must develop an impartial and appropriate factual record upon which to make findings on the claims raised by the complaint. An appropriate factual record is defined as one that allows a reasonable fact finder to draw conclusions as to whether discrimination occurred.

The investigation must be completed within 180 days from the filing of the complaint. A copy of the investigative file must be provided to the complainant, along with a notification that, within 30 days of receipt of the file, the complainant has the right to request a hearing and a decision from an EEOC Administrative Judge, or may request an immediate final decision from the agency.

Offer of Resolution

An agency may make an offer of resolution to a complainant who is represented by an attorney at any time after the filing of a complaint, but not later than the date an administrative judge is appointed to conduct a hearing. An administrative judge is an EEOC employee who independently decides discrimination complaints of federal employees.

An agency may make an offer of resolution to a complaint, represented by an attorney or not, after the parties have received notice that an administrative judge has been appointed to conduct a hearing, but not later than 30 days prior to a hearing.

Such offer of resolution must be in writing and include a notice explaining the possible consequences of failing to accept the offer. If the complainant fails to accept the offer within 30 days of receipt, and the relief awarded in the final decision on the complaint is not more favorable than the offer, then the complainant shall not receive payment from the agency of attorney's fees or costs incurred after the expiration of the 30-day acceptance period.

Amending the Complaint

A complainant may amend a complaint at any time prior to the conclusion of the investigation to include issues or claims like or related to those raised in the complaint. After requesting a hearing, a complainant may file a motion with the administrative judge to amend a complaint to include issues or claims like or related to those raised in the complaint.

Dismissing the Complaint

Prior to a request for a hearing, in lieu of accepting a complaint for investigation, an agency may dismiss an entire complaint for any of the following reasons:

1. Failure to state a claim, or stating the same claim that is pending or has been decided by the agency or the EEOC;

2. Failure to comply with the time limits;

3. Filing a complaint on a matter that has not been brought to the attention of an EEO counselor and which is not like or related to the matters counseled;

4. Filing a complaint which is the basis of a pending civil action, or which was the basis of a civil action already decided by a court;

5. Where the complainant has already elected to pursue the matter through either a collective bargaining negotiated grievance procedure, or in an appeal to the Merit Systems Protection Board;

6. Where the matter is moot or merely alleges a proposal to take a personnel action;

7. Where the complainant cannot be located;

8. Where the complainant fails to respond to a request to provide relevant information;

9. Where the complaint alleges dissatisfaction with the processing of a previously filed complaint; and

10. Where the complaint is part of a clear pattern of misuse of the EEO process for a purpose other than the prevention and elimination of employment discrimination.

If an agency believes that some, but not all, of the claims in a complaint should be dismissed for the above reasons, it must notify the complainant in writing of the rationale for this determination, identify the allegations which will not be investigated, and place a copy of this notice in the investigative file. This determination is reviewable by the EEOC administrative judge if a hearing is requested on the remainder of the complaint, but is not appealable until final action is taken by the agency on the remainder of the complaint.

Discovery

Prior to the administrative hearing, the parties may conduct discovery. The purpose of discovery is to enable a party to obtain relevant information for preparation of the party's case. Each party initially bears their own costs for discovery. If the administrative judge determines that the agency failed to complete its investigation in a timely manner, or failed to adequately investigate the allegations, it may require the agency to bear the costs for the complainant to obtain depositions or other discovery.

Administrative Hearing

Requests for an administrative hearing must be sent by the complainant to the EEOC office indicated in the agency's acknowledgment letter, with a copy to the agency's EEO office. Within 15 days of receipt of the request for a hearing, the agency must provide a copy of the complaint file to the EEOC. The EEOC will then appoint an administrative judge to conduct a hearing.

An administrative hearing is similar to a trial before a judge at the courthouse. As the presiding official, the administrative judge acts as both the judge and jury. Proceedings, for the most part, are informal. Parties are generally permitted to make opening and closing statements; offer evidence, such as witness testimony and documents; examine and cross-examine witnesses; and raise objections and obtain rulings on objections from the administrative judge.

The complainant is not required to retain an attorney or have any other person represent them. They may proceed "pro se"—i.e., act as their own attorney. Nevertheless, the complainant is expected to be familiar with EEOC rules of practice and procedure and be prepared at the hearing. At the hearing, the complainant is required to proceed first with presentation of evidence that supports their allegations of discrimination. At all times, the complainant carries the ultimate burden of proving their case with relevant and material evidence.

Given the importance of the hearing, a complainant may be better advised to retain an attorney or designate a knowledgeable co-worker, union official or other individual as their representative in the case. If so, the complainant is expected to act through their representative. In addition, a successful complainant is ineligible to receive reasonable attorney's fees as part of any award in the case unless he or she is represented by an attorney.

Hearings are considered part of the investigative process, and are closed to the public. The administrative judge conducts the hearing and receives relevant information or documents as evidence. The hearing is recorded and the agency is responsible for paying for the transcripts of the hearing. Rules of evidence are not strictly applied to the proceedings. If the administrative judge determines that some or all of the facts are not in genuine dispute, he or she may limit the scope of the hearing or issue a decision without a hearing.

The administrative judge must conduct the hearing and issue a decision on the complaint within 180 days of receipt of the complaint file from the agency. The administrative judge will send copies of the hearing record, the transcript, and the decision to the parties.

Final Agency Action

After the administrative judge has issued a decision, the agency must take final action on the complaint by issuing a final order within 40 days of receipt of the hearing record and the decision. If the agency does not issue a final order within 40 days after receiving the administrative judge's decision, the decision becomes the final order of the agency.

The agency's final order must notify the complainant whether or not the agency will fully implement the decision, and shall contain notice of the complainant's right to appeal to the EEOC or to file a civil action. If the final order does not fully implement the decision, the agency must simultaneously file an appeal with the EEOC, and attach a copy of the appeal to the final order.

When an administrative judge has not issued a decision, the agency must take final action by issuing a final decision. The agency's final decision will consist of findings by the agency on the merits of each issue in the complaint. The agency's decision must be issued within 60 days of receiving notification that the complainant has requested an immediate final decision. The agency's decision must contain notice of the complainant's right to appeal to the EEOC, or to file a civil action in federal court.

Filing an Appeal with the EEOC

A dissatisfied complainant may appeal an agency's final action to the EEOC within 30 days of receiving the agency's decision. The agency may appeal a decision by an EEOC administrative judge within 40 days of receiving the administrative judge's decision.

On class complaints, a class agent may appeal an agency's final decision on the merits of the class complaint within 30 days from receipt, or a class member may appeal the final decision on his or her claim for individual relief within 30 days from receipt of the final decision.

If the complaint is a "mixed case," the complainant may appeal the final agency decision to the MSPB or ask the MSPB for a hearing. Once the MSPB issues its decision on the complaint, the complainant may petition the EEOC for review of the MSPB decision concerning the discrimination claim.

Appeals must be filed with the EEOC's Office of Federal Operations (OFO). Any statement or brief on behalf of a complainant in support of an appeal must be submitted to the OFO within 30 days of filing the notice of appeal. Any statement or brief on behalf of the agency in support of its appeal must be filed within 20 days of filing the notice of appeal.

The agency must submit the complaint file to the OFO within 30 days of initial notification that the complainant has filed an appeal, or within

30 days of submission of an appeal by the agency. Any statement or brief in opposition to an appeal must be submitted to the OFO and served on the opposing party within 30 days of receipt of the statement or brief supporting the appeal, or, if no statement or brief supporting the appeal has been filed, within 60 days of receipt of the appeal.

The EEOC has the authority to draw adverse inferences against a party for failing to comply with its appeal procedures or requests for information. The EEOC's decision will be based on a preponderance of the evidence. The decision will also inform the complainant of his or her right to file a civil action.

Filing a Civil Action

Prior to filing a civil action under Title VII or the Rehabilitation Act of 1973, a federal sector complainant must first exhaust the administrative process set forth above. Under the Age Discrimination in Employment Act (ADEA), a complainant may proceed directly to federal court after giving the EEOC their notice of intent to sue. Under the Equal Pay Act, a complainant may file a civil action within 2 years, or 3 years for willful violations, regardless of whether he or she has pursued an administrative complaint. Filing a civil action terminates any appeal before the EEOC.

Class Complaints

A class complaint may begin as an individual complaint of discrimination. At a certain point, it may become evident that there are many more individuals than the complainant affected by the issues raised in the individual complaint. A complainant may move for class certification at any reasonable point in the process when it becomes apparent that there are class implications to the claims raised in the individual complaint.

Class complaints of discrimination are processed differently from individual complaints. The employee or applicant who wishes to file a class complaint must first seek counseling and be counseled, just like an individual complaint. However, once counseling is completed, the class complaint is not investigated by the respondent agency. Rather, the complaint is forwarded to the nearest EEOC Field or District Office, where an EEOC administrative judge is appointed to make decision as to whether to accept or dismiss the class complaint.

The administrative judge examines the class to determine whether it meets the class certification requirements of:

1. Numerosity;
2. Commonality;

3. Typicality; and
4. Adequacy of representation.

The administrative judge may issue a decision dismissing the class because it fails to meet any of these class certification requirements, as well as for any of the reasons for dismissal for individual complaints discussed above.

The administrative judge transmits his or her decision to accept or dismiss a class complaint to the class agent and the agency. The agency must then take final action by issuing a final order within 40 days of receipt of the decision. The final order must notify the agent whether or not the agency will implement the decision.

If the agency's final order does not implement the decision, the agency must simultaneously appeal the decision to the OFO. A copy of the agency's appeal must be attached to the agency's final order.

The dismissal of a class complaint shall inform the class agent either: (1) that the complaint is being filed on that date as an individual complaint and processed accordingly; or (2) that the complaint is also dismissed as an individual complaint for one of the reasons for dismissal discussed above. In addition, a dismissal must inform the class agent of the right to appeal to the OFO, or to file a civil action in federal court.

When a class complaint is accepted, the agency must use reasonable means to notify the class members of the following: (1) acceptance of the class complaint; (2) a description of the issues accepted as part of the complaint; (3) an explanation of the binding nature of the final decision or resolution on the class members; and (4) the name, address and telephone number of the class representative.

In lieu of an investigation by the respondent agency, the EEOC administrative judge develops the record through discovery and a hearing. The administrative judge then issues a recommended decision to the agency. Within 60 days of receipt of the recommended decision on the merits of the class complaint, the agency must issue a final decision that either accepts, rejects or modifies the recommended decision. If the agency fails to issue such a decision within that time frame, the recommended decision becomes the agency's final decision in the class complaint.

When discrimination is found in the final decision, and a class member believes that he or she is entitled to relief, the class member may file a written claim with the agency within 30 days of receipt of notification by the agency of its final decision. The claim for relief must contain a specific showing that the claimant is a class member entitled to relief. The administrative judge retains jurisdiction over the complaint in order to resolve disputed claims by class members.

When a finding of discrimination against a class has been made, there is a presumption of discrimination as to each member of the class. Thus, the agency must show by clear and convincing evidence that any class member is not entitled to relief. The agency must issue a final decision on each individual claim for relief within 90 days of filing. Such decision may be appealed to the OFO, or a civil action may be filed in federal court.

A class complaint may be resolved at any time by agreement between the agency and the class agent. Notice of such a resolution must be provided to all class members, and reviewed and approved by the administrative judge.

If the administrative judge finds that the proposed resolution is not fair to the class as a whole, then he or she will issue a decision vacating the agreement, and may replace the class agent with some other eligible class member to further process the class complaint. If the administrative judge finds that the resolution is fair to the class as a whole, the resolution is binding on all class members.

CHAPTER 3: THE EEOC MEDIATION PROGRAM

HISTORY OF THE EEOC MEDIATION PROGRAM

In 1991, the EEOC began pilot mediation programs in four of its field offices located in Philadelphia, New Orleans, Houston, and Washington, DC. Subsequently, pilot programs were established in all District offices. Based on the success of the pilot programs, the Commission concluded that mediation was a viable alternative to the traditional investigatory methods used by the EEOC to resolve charges of employment discrimination, and that an ADR program should be implemented. The EEOC mediation program was fully implemented by April 1999.

The EEOC mediation program is administered primarily through its field offices, including the Washington Field Office and 24 District Offices, located throughout the country. Each field office has a staff member who is responsible for coordinating mediation activities for discrimination charges filed within that office's geographical jurisdiction.

A directory of the EEOC Mediation Program Offices is set forth in Appendix 8.

Since its inception, the EEOC mediation program has been very successful in resolving charges of employment discrimination. Several studies have been conducted by independent researchers to evaluate the program's effectiveness and to identify potential improvements. One survey found that parties who participated in mediation were very satisfied with the process, and that 96% of employers and 91% of charging parties would use the mediation program again if offered. From 1999 through 2003, over 52,400 mediations have been held and more than 35,100 charges (69%) have been successfully resolved in an average of 85 days.

A table of EEOC mediation statistics (1999–2003) is set forth in Appendix 9.

WHAT IS MEDIATION?

Mediation is a form of alternative dispute resolution (ADR) that is offered by the EEOC as an alternative to the traditional investigative or litigation process. Participation in the mediation program is confidential, voluntary, and requires consent from both the charging party and employer.

Mediation is an informal process in which a neutral third party—known as a mediator—assists the opposing parties in reaching a voluntary, negotiated resolution of a charge of discrimination. Only mediators who are experienced and trained in mediation and equal employment opportunity law are assigned to mediate EEOC charges. EEOC has a staff of trained mediators and also contracts with professional external mediators to mediate charges filed with the EEOC. All EEOC mediators, whether internal staff or external mediators, are neutral unbiased professionals with no stake in the outcome of the mediation process.

Mediation gives the parties the opportunity to discuss the issues raised in the charge, clear up misunderstandings, determine the underlying interests or concerns, find areas of agreement and, ultimately, to incorporate those areas of agreements into resolutions. A mediator does not resolve the charge or impose a decision on the parties. Instead, the mediator helps the parties to agree on a mutually acceptable resolution.

Eligibility

All charges are not eligible for mediation. The EEOC evaluates each charge to determine whether it is appropriate for mediation considering such factors as: (1) the nature of the case; (2) the relationship of the parties; (3) the size and complexity of the case; and (4) the relief sought by the charging party. Charges that the EEOC has determined to be without merit are not eligible for mediation.

Confidentiality

The EEOC maintains strict confidentiality in its mediation program. The mediator and the parties must sign agreements that they will keep everything that is revealed during the mediation confidential. The mediation sessions are not tape-recorded or transcribed. Notes taken during the mediation by the mediator are subsequently destroyed.

Information disclosed during mediation is not revealed to anyone, including other EEOC employees. Settlement agreements secured during mediation do not constitute an admission by the employer of any violation of the law.

Further, in order to ensure confidentiality, the mediation program is insulated from the EEOC's investigative and litigation functions. The EEOC mediators only mediate charges. They are precluded from performing any other functions related to the investigation or litigation of charges.

Representation

It is not necessary to have an attorney or other representative in order to participate in the EEOC mediation program, however, either party may choose to do so. The mediator will decide what role the attorney or representative will play during the mediation. For example, the mediator may ask that they provide advice and counsel, but not speak for a party. If a party plans to bring an attorney or other representative to the mediation session, he or she can discuss this with the mediator prior to the mediation session.

Enforceability

An agreement reached during mediation is enforceable in court just like any other settlement agreement resolving a charge of discrimination filed with the EEOC. If either party believes that the other party has failed to comply with a mediated settlement agreement, he or she should contact the ADR Coordinator.

THE MEDIATION PROCESS

The EEOC investigation process begins after the charge has been filed. The employer is notified that the charge has been filed. Prior to beginning the formal investigation, a case may be selected for the EEOC mediation program. Mediation will usually be offered early in the processing of the charge, as an alternative to a lengthy investigation. The majority of mediations are completed in one session, which usually lasts from one to five hours. There is no cost to the parties in selecting the mediation process.

If a case is selected for mediation, an EEOC representative will contact the employee and employer concerning their interest in participating in the program. If both parties agree, a mediation session is scheduled.

The charging party and a representative of the employer attend the mediation session. The person representing the employer should be familiar with the facts of the charge and have the authority to settle the charge on behalf of the employer.

If a charge is not resolved during the mediation process, the charge is returned to an investigative unit, and continues to be processed and investigated just like any other charge. Because the entire mediation process is strictly confidential, information revealed during the mediation session cannot be disclosed to anyone and thus cannot be used during any subsequent investigation.

USING MEDIATION AT THE CONCILIATION STAGE

In order to increase opportunities for mediation, the EEOC has expanded the charges eligible for mediation and now mediation is available at the conciliation stage, after a finding of discrimination has been issued, in appropriate cases. However, if mediation occurs at the conciliation stage, the EEOC joins in as a participant along with the charging party and respondent.

Either party can request mediation without an offer from the EEOC. As long as both parties agree to participate, the EEOC will consider the charge for mediation.

ADVANTAGES OF MEDIATION

Mediation has a number of advantages over filing a discrimination charge or pursuing a private civil lawsuit:

1. Mediation is available at no cost to the parties.

2. Mediation is fair and neutral. The parties have an equal say in the process, and decide the settlement terms, not the mediator. There is no determination of guilt or innocence in the process.

3. Mediation saves time and money. Mediation usually occurs in the charge process, and many mediations are completed in one meeting.

4. Mediation does not require legal or other representation, which is optional but not required.

5. Mediation is confidential. All parties sign a confidentiality agreement. Information disclosed during mediation is not revealed to anyone, including other EEOC investigative or legal staff.

6. Mediation avoids lengthy litigation. In addition, mediation costs less than a lawsuit and avoids the uncertainty of judicial outcome.

7. Mediation encourages cooperation between the parties. Mediation fosters a problem solving approach to complaints, thus, workplace disruptions are reduced. With investigation, even if the charge is dismissed by the EEOC, the underlying problems may remain, affecting others in the workforce and human resources staff. During mediation, the parties share information, which can lead to a better understanding of issues affecting the workplace.

8. Mediation improves communication. Mediation provides a neutral and confidential setting where both parties can openly discuss their views on the underlying dispute. Enhanced communication can lead to mutually satisfactory resolutions.

9. The parties to mediation design their own solution. A neutral third party—the mediator—assists the parties in reaching a voluntary, mutually beneficial resolution. Mediation can resolve all issues important to the parties, not just the underlying legal dispute.

10. Mediation has a proven success rate. An independent survey showed 96% of all respondents and 91% of all charging parties who used mediation would use it again if offered.

THE EEOC "REFERRAL BACK" MEDIATION PILOT PROGRAM

Some employers have adopted internal programs for informally resolving employment disputes internally, including discrimination claims. Such programs have assisted in the resolution of claims promptly and amicably

The EEOC has initiated a mediation pilot program to explore whether employer-provided dispute resolution programs that operate fairly and voluntarily can serve as an effective means of resolving employment discrimination charges filed with the EEOC. The charges eligible for the pilot program are the same charges eligible for the EEOC private sector mediation program.

Participation Criteria

The EEOC reviews employer plans to determine whether they meet the criteria for participation in this pilot program. The general criteria the EEOC has established for the employer's program to be considered for participation in the pilot program include the following:

1. The employee's participation is voluntary.

2. The employer has clearly written procedures that have been communicated to employees.

3. The program is free to the employee.

4. The program addresses claims and provides the relief available under EEOC statutes.

5. Settlements are in writing and enforceable in court.

In addition, the employer's program must be an established program. To be considered established, an employer must demonstrate:

1. That employees have used the internal ADR program for EEO related disputes;

2. That the employer has recently and effectively informed employees of the existence of its ADR program, or the employer must agree, in coordination with the EEOC, to publicize its participation in the pilot program.

Pilot Program Procedure

Under the pilot program, a charging party who has filed a charge with EEOC may elect to have his or her charge referred to the employer's program in an attempt to resolve the dispute. Participation by the charging party is completely voluntary. If the charging party decides not to participate in the pilot program, this decision will not affect the further processing of their charge by the EEOC.

If the charging party elects to participate in the pilot program, the EEOC will suspend processing of the charge for up to 60 days, until the matter has been resolved, or until the charging party requests that the EEOC resume processing. If the dispute is resolved through the employer's program, the charge will be closed. If the dispute is not resolved, the EEOC will resume processing of the charge. The processing of the charge, however, will not be suspended a second time, even if the charging party requests or re-enters the employer's internal program.

Confidentiality Agreements

The EEOC will honor a confidentiality agreement voluntarily entered into by the parties participating in the pilot program. However, the EEOC is not prevented from using otherwise confidential information under such an agreement, if it was obtained by the EEOC from other independent sources or through any subsequent EEOC investigation of the charge.

Settlement Agreements

Any settlement agreement reached in the pilot program must be in writing. The EEOC will honor a written agreement resolving the charges handled through the program, however, the EEOC will not participate in drafting or signing the agreement.

UNIVERSAL AGREEMENT TO MEDIATE (UAM)

A Universal Agreement to Mediate (UAM) is an agreement between the EEOC and an employer to mediate all eligible charges filed against the employer, prior to an agency investigation or litigation. A UAM substitutes for the individual agreement to mediate which the parties sign prior to a mediation being conducted. Because mediation is voluntary, the employer or the charging party may opt out of mediation on a particular charge even though a UAM has been signed.

UAMs may be local, regional, or national. Local UAMs are agreements that exist between an employer and a particular EEOC field office to mediate eligible charges filed against that employer within the field office's geographic jurisdiction. Regional and National UAMs are agreements between an employer and the EEOC to mediate all of an employer's eligible charges in a multi-state region or on a nationwide basis.

Benefits of a UAM

The benefits of signing a UAM include the following:

1. A UAM demonstrates from the outset a company's willingness to mediate on cases eligible for mediation, which may contribute to the ultimate satisfactory resolution of a matter.
2. With a UAM, the initial step of contacting the employer to see if they will mediate a particular charge is shortened or eliminated.
3. A UAM establishes a point of contact for the employer, thereby expediting the flow of information between the EEOC and the employer.
4. Fast tracking the information through established contact points expedites the scheduling of a mediation session.
5. UAMs are flexible. They allow parties to opt out of mediation on a case-by-case basis if either believes the claim is not appropriate.

A sample Universal Agreement to Mediate is set forth in Appendix 10.

Signatories

At the end of fiscal year 2006, the EEOC had signed 957 local UAMS, and 142 Regional and National UAMs, for a total of 1099. UAMs are confidential unless an employer has agreed to make the agreement public. Certain employers have given the EEOC permission to include them on the EEOC list of National Universal Agreements to Mediate.

A list of signatories to the National Universal Agreement to Mediate with the EEOC Mediation Program is set forth in Appendix 11.

CHAPTER 4: DISCRIMINATION ON THE BASIS OF RACE OR COLOR

IN GENERAL

Title VII of the Civil Rights Act of 1964 protects individuals against employment discrimination on the basis of race and color, making it unlawful to discriminate against any employee or applicant for employment because of his or her race or color, in regard to hiring, termination, promotion, compensation, job training, or any other term, condition, or privilege of employment.

Title VII also prohibits employment decisions based on stereotypes and assumptions about abilities, traits, or the performance of individuals of certain racial groups. Title VII prohibits both intentional discrimination and neutral job policies that disproportionately exclude minorities and that are not job related.

Further, equal employment opportunity cannot be denied because of:

1. Marriage to, or association with, an individual of a different race;
2. Membership in, or association with, ethnic based organizations or groups; or
3. Attendance or participation in schools or places of worship generally associated with certain minority groups.

RACE-RELATED CHARACTERISTICS AND CONDITIONS

Discrimination on the basis of an immutable characteristic associated with race, such as skin color, hair texture, or certain facial features violates Title VII, even though not all members of the race share the same characteristic.

Title VII also prohibits discrimination on the basis of a condition that predominantly affects one race, unless the practice is job-related and consistent with business necessity. For example, since sickle cell anemia predominantly occurs in African-Americans, a policy that excludes individuals with sickle cell anemia must be job-related and consistent with business necessity.

PRE-EMPLOYMENT INQUIRIES CONCERNING RACE OR COLOR

Requesting pre-employment information that discloses or tends to disclose an applicant's race suggests that race will be unlawfully used as a basis for hiring. Solicitation of such pre-employment information is presumed to be a basis for making selection decisions. Therefore, if members of minority groups were excluded from employment, the request for such pre-employment information would likely constitute evidence of discrimination under Title VII.

Nevertheless, employers may need information about their employees' or applicants' race for legitimate reasons, such as for affirmative action purposes. One way to obtain racial information and simultaneously guard against discriminatory selection is for employers to use separate forms or otherwise keep the information about an applicant's race separate from the application. In that way, the employer can capture the information it needs but ensure that it is not used in the selection decision.

The EEOC suggests that employers who have a legitimate reason for requesting this information utilize a system whereby the applicant's racial identification is placed on a "tear-off-sheet" which is separated from the application once it is completed, and is not used in the selection process.

JOB REQUIREMENTS

Job requirements must be uniformly and consistently applied to persons of all races and colors. Even if a job requirement is applied consistently, if it is not important for job performance or business needs, the requirement may be found unlawful if it excludes persons of a certain racial group or color significantly more than others.

Examples of potentially unlawful practices include:

1. Soliciting applications only from sources in which all or most potential workers are of the same race or color;

2. Requiring applicants to have a certain educational background that is not important for job performance or business needs;

3. Testing applicants for knowledge, skills or abilities that are not important for job performance or business needs.

COMPENSATION AND OTHER EMPLOYMENT TERMS

Title VII prohibits discrimination in compensation and other terms, conditions, and privileges of employment. Thus, race or color discrimination may not be the basis for differences in pay or benefits, work assignments, performance evaluations, training, discipline or discharge, or any other area of employment.

SEGREGATION AND CLASSIFICATION OF EMPLOYEES

Title VII is violated where employees who belong to a protected group are segregated by physically isolating them from other employees or from customer contact. In addition, employers may not assign employees according to race or color. For example, Title VII prohibits assigning primarily African-Americans to predominantly African-American establishments or geographic areas.

It is also illegal to exclude members of one group from particular positions, or to group or categorize employees or jobs so that certain jobs are primarily held by members of a certain protected group.

In addition, coding applications and resumes to designate an applicant's race, by either an employer or employment agency, constitutes evidence of discrimination where people of a certain race or color are excluded from employment or from certain positions.

HARASSMENT

Harassment on the basis of race and/or color violates Title VII. Ethnic slurs, so-called racial jokes, offensive or derogatory comments, or other verbal or physical conduct based on an individual's race or color constitutes unlawful harassment if the conduct creates an intimidating, hostile, or offensive working environment, or if it interferes with the individual's work performance.

To constitute harassment, the conduct has to be unwelcome and offensive, and has to be severe or pervasive. Employers are required to take appropriate steps to prevent and correct unlawful harassment. Likewise, employees are responsible for reporting harassment at an early stage to prevent its escalation.

RETALIATION

Employees have a right to be free from retaliation for their opposition to discrimination. Thus, it is a violation of Title VII for an employer to retaliate against an individual for opposing employment practices that discriminate based on race or color, or for filing a discrimination charge, testifying, or participating in any way in an investigation, proceeding, or litigation under Title VII.

STATISTICS

In 2006, the EEOC received 27,238 charges of race discrimination. The EEOC resolved 25,992 race charges in 2006, and recovered $61.4 million in monetary benefits for charging parties and other aggrieved individuals, not including monetary benefits obtained through litigation.

A table of race-based discrimination charges and resolutions (2000–2006) is set forth in Appendix 12.

CHAPTER 5: DISCRIMINATION ON THE BASIS OF RELIGION

IN GENERAL

Title VII of the Civil Rights Act of 1964 protects individuals against employment discrimination on the basis of religion. Title VII makes it unlawful to discriminate against any employee or applicant for employment because of his or her religion, in regard to hiring, termination, promotion, compensation, job training, or any other term, condition, or privilege of employment. Thus, if you are fired or laid off because of your religious beliefs or affiliation, you are protected under Title VII. In addition, an employer may not treat employees or applicants either less or more favorably because of their religious beliefs or practices.

WHAT CONSTITUTES RELIGIOUS BELIEF OR PRACTICE?

In most cases, whether or not a practice or belief is religious is not at issue in a Title VII case. However, in those cases in which the issue does exist, the EEOC will define religious practices to include moral or ethical beliefs as to what is right and wrong which are sincerely held with the strength of traditional religious views.

The fact that no religious group espouses such beliefs, or the fact that the religious group to which the individual professes to belong may not accept such belief will not determine whether the belief is a religious belief of the employee or prospective employee.

In addition, an employee cannot be fired for engaging in religious expression if employees are permitted to engage in other types of personal expression at work, unless the religious expression would impose an undue hardship on the employer. Therefore, an employer may not place more restrictions on religious expression than on other forms of expression that have a comparable effect on workplace efficiency.

PRE-EMPLOYMENT INQUIRIES

The EEOC has concluded that the use of pre-selection inquiries that determine an applicant's availability has an exclusionary effect on the employment opportunities of persons with certain religious practices. The use of such inquiries will, therefore, be considered to violate Title VII unless the employer can show that:

1. The inquiry did not have an exclusionary effect on its employees or prospective employees needing an accommodation for the same religious practices; or

2. The inquiry was otherwise justified by business necessity.

The burden is on the employer to demonstrate that factors other than the need for an accommodation were the reason for rejecting the qualified applicant, or that a reasonable accommodation without undue hardship was not possible.

REASONABLE ACCOMMODATION

Under Title VII, an employer or labor organization has a duty to reasonably accommodate the religious practices of an employee or prospective employee, unless the employer demonstrates that accommodation would result in undue hardship on the conduct of its business.

A reasonable religious accommodation is any adjustment to the work environment that will allow the employee to practice his religion. Flexible scheduling, voluntary substitutions, job reassignments, lateral transfers, and modifying workplace practices, policies and/or procedures are examples of how an employer might accommodate an employee's religious beliefs.

Examples of religious practices or beliefs that may require an accommodation include:

1. Observance of a Sabbath or religious holiday;

2. Need for prayer break during working hours;

3. Practice of following certain dietary requirements;

4. Practice of not working during a mourning period for a deceased relative;

5. Prohibition against medical examinations;

6. Prohibition against membership in labor and other organizations; and

7. Practices concerning dress and other personal grooming habits.

Thus, for example, employers cannot schedule medical examinations in conflict with a current or prospective employee's belief, maintain a restrictive dress code, or refuse to allow observance of a Sabbath or religious holiday, unless the employer can prove that this would cause the employer an undue hardship.

ALTERNATIVE REASONABLE ACCOMMODATIONS

When there is more than one method of accommodation available that would not cause undue hardship, the EEOC will determine whether the accommodation offered is reasonable by examining:

1. The alternatives for accommodation considered by the employer or labor organization; and

2. The alternatives for accommodation, if any, actually offered to the individual requiring accommodation.

Some alternatives for accommodating religious practices might disadvantage the individual with respect to his or her employment opportunities, such as compensation, terms, conditions, or privileges of employment. Therefore, when there is more than one means of accommodation that would not cause undue hardship, the employer or labor organization must offer the alternative which least disadvantages the individual with respect to his or her employment opportunities.

The EEOC suggests that flexible scheduling, voluntary substitutions, job reassignments and lateral transfers are examples of ways an employer can accommodate an employee's religious beliefs.

UNDUE HARDSHIP

An employer is not required to accommodate an employee's religious beliefs and practices if doing so would impose an undue hardship on the employer's legitimate business interests. An employer can claim undue hardship when accommodating an employee's religious practices, if allowing such practices requires "more than a de minimis cost."

The EEOC will determine what constitutes "more than a de minimis cost" taking into consideration the identifiable cost in relation to the size and operating cost of the employer, and the number of individuals who will in fact need a particular accommodation.

For example, an employer can show undue hardship if accommodating an employee's religious practices requires more than ordinary administrative costs, diminishes efficiency in other jobs, infringes on other employees' job rights or benefits, impairs workplace safety, causes co-workers to carry the accommodated employee's share of potentially hazardous or burdensome work, or if the proposed accommodation conflicts with another law or regulation.

In addition, undue hardship may also be shown if changing a bona fide seniority system to accommodate one employee's religious practices denies another employee the job or shift preference guaranteed by the seniority system.

UNION DUES

Some collective bargaining agreements include a provision that each employee must join the labor organization or pay the labor organization a sum equivalent to dues. When an employee's religious practices do not permit compliance with such a provision, the labor organization should accommodate the employee by not requiring the employee to join the organization and by permitting him or her to donate a sum equivalent to dues to a charitable organization.

MANDATORY "NEW AGE" TRAINING PROGRAMS

Mandatory "new age" training programs, designed to improve employee motivation, cooperation or productivity through meditation, yoga, biofeedback or other practices, may conflict with the non-discriminatory provisions of Title VII.

Employers must accommodate any employee who gives notice that these programs are inconsistent with the employee's religious beliefs, whether or not the employer believes there is a religious basis for the employee's objection.

HARASSMENT

Employers must take steps to prevent religious harassment of their employees. An employer can reduce the chance that employees will engage in unlawful religious harassment by implementing an anti-harassment policy, and having an effective procedure for reporting, investigating and correcting harassing conduct.

RETALIATION

It is unlawful to retaliate against an individual for opposing employment practices that discriminate based on religion, or for filing a discrimination charge, testifying, or participating in any way in an investigation, proceeding, or litigation under Title VII.

STATISTICS

In 2006, the EEOC received 2,541 charges of religious discrimination. The EEOC resolved 2,387 religious discrimination charges in 2006, and recovered $5.7 million in monetary benefits for charging parties and other aggrieved individuals, not including monetary benefits obtained through litigation.

A table of religion-based discrimination charges and resolutions (2000–2006) is set forth in Appendix 13.

CHAPTER 6: DISCRIMINATION ON THE BASIS OF SEX

IN GENERAL

Title VII of the Civil Rights Act of 1964 protects individuals against employment discrimination on the basis of sex, making it unlawful to discriminate against any employee or applicant for employment because of his or her sex, in regard to hiring, termination, promotion, compensation, job training, or any other term, condition, or privilege of employment.

This principle of nondiscrimination requires that individuals be considered on the basis of individual capacities and not on the basis of any characteristics generally attributed to the group. Thus, the following sex-based employment decisions would violate Title VII:

1. The refusal to hire a woman because of her sex based on the assumptions of the comparative employment characteristics of women in general, such as the high turnover rate among women as opposed to men;

2. The refusal to hire an individual based on stereotyped characterizations of the sexes. For example, the notion that a woman is less capable of aggressive salesmanship than a man; and

3. The refusal to hire an individual because of the preferences of coworkers, the employer, clients or customers.

Sex as a Bona Fide Occupational Qualification

Labeling a particular job a "man's job" or a "woman's job" tends to unnecessarily deny employment opportunities to one sex or the other. Thus, the EEOC believes that the "bona fide occupational qualification" exception as to sex should be interpreted narrowly.

Nevertheless, where it is necessary for the purpose of authenticity or genuineness to the position, the EEOC will consider sex to be a bona fide occupational qualification. For example, if an acting role requires an actor to play a male part as opposed to an actress, the sexual preference would be considered a bona fide occupational qualification.

Gender-Oriented State Laws

Many states have enacted laws or promulgated administrative regulations with respect to the employment of females. Among these laws are those which prohibit or limit the employment of females, e.g. the employment of females in certain occupations, in jobs requiring the lifting or carrying of weights exceeding certain prescribed limits, during certain hours of the night, for more than a specified number of hours per day or per week, and for certain periods of time before and after childbirth.

The EEOC has found that such laws and regulations do not take into account the capacities, preferences, and abilities of individual females and, therefore, discriminate on the basis of sex. Thus, the EEOC has concluded that such laws and regulations conflict with and are superseded by Title VII. Therefore, such laws will not be considered a defense to an otherwise established unlawful employment practice or as a basis for the application of the bona fide occupational qualification exception.

In addition, the EEOC has concluded that state laws and regulations which discriminate on the basis of sex with regard to the employment of minors are in conflict with, and are superseded by Title VII, to the extent that such laws are more restrictive for one sex. Accordingly, restrictions on the employment of minors of one sex over and above those imposed on minors of the other sex will not be considered a defense to an otherwise established unlawful employment practice or as a basis for the application of the bona fide occupational qualification exception.

A number of states require that minimum wage and premium pay for overtime be provided for female employees. An employer will be deemed to have engaged in an unlawful employment practice if:

1. It refuses to hire or otherwise adversely affects the employment opportunities of female applicants or employees in order to avoid the payment of minimum wages or overtime pay required by State law; or

2. It does not provide the same benefits for male employees.

As to other kinds of sex-oriented state employment laws, such as those requiring special rest and meal periods or physical facilities for women, provision of these benefits to one sex only will be a violation of Title VII.

Thus, an employer will be deemed to have engaged in an unlawful employment practice if:

1. It refuses to hire or otherwise adversely affects the employment opportunities of female applicants or employees in order to avoid the provision of such benefits; or

2. It does not provide the same benefits for male employees.

If the employer can prove that business necessity precludes providing these benefits to both men and women, then the state law is in conflict with and superseded by Title VII as to that employer. In such a situation, the employer shall not provide such benefits to members of either sex.

Some states require that separate restrooms be provided for employees of each sex. An employer will be deemed to have engaged in an unlawful employment practice if it refuses to hire or otherwise adversely affects the employment opportunities of applicants or employees in order to avoid the provision of such restrooms for persons of that sex.

Separate Lines of Progression and Seniority Systems

Under Title VII, it is an unlawful employment practice to classify a job as "male" or "female," or to maintain separate lines of progression or separate seniority lists based on sex, where this would adversely affect any employee unless sex is a bona fide occupational qualification for that job.

Accordingly, employment practices are unlawful which arbitrarily classify jobs so that:

1. A female is prohibited from applying for a job labeled "male," or for a job in a "male" line of progression; and vice versa;

2. A male scheduled for layoff is prohibited from displacing a less senior female on a "female" seniority list; and vice versa.

A seniority system or line of progression which distinguishes between "light" and "heavy" jobs constitutes an unlawful employment practice if it operates as a disguised form of classification by sex, or creates unreasonable obstacles to the advancement by members of either sex into jobs which members of that sex would reasonably be expected to perform.

Discrimination Against Married Women

The EEOC has determined that an employer's rule which forbids or restricts the employment of married women, and which is not applicable to married men, is a discrimination based on sex prohibited by Title VII.

Advertising Job Opportunities

It is a violation of Title VII for a help-wanted advertisement to indicate a preference, limitation, specification, or discrimination based on sex unless sex is a bona fide occupational qualification for the particular job involved. The placement of an advertisement in columns classified by publishers on the basis of sex, such as columns headed "Male" or "Female," will be considered an expression of a preference, limitation, specification, or discrimination based on sex.

Employment Agencies

It is unlawful for an employment agency to discriminate against any individual because of sex. The EEOC has determined that private employment agencies that deal exclusively with one sex are engaged in an unlawful employment practice, except to the extent that such agencies limit their services to furnishing employees for particular jobs for which sex is a bona fide occupational qualification.

If an employment agency receives a job order containing an unlawful sex specification, it will share responsibility with the employer who placed the job order if the agency fills the order knowing that the sex specification is not based upon a bona fide occupational qualification.

However, if an employment agency believes that the employer's claim of bona fide occupational qualification has substance, the agency will not be responsible regardless of the EEOC's determination as to the employer. Thus, the employment agency is advised to maintain a written record of each such job order, including the name of the employer, the description of the job, and the basis for the employer's claim of bona fide occupational qualification.

Pre-employment Inquiries

Although a pre-employment inquiry may ask whether the applicant is "male" or "female," or "Mr., Mrs., or Miss," the inquiry must be made in good faith for a nondiscriminatory purpose. Any pre-employment inquiry in connection with prospective employment that expresses—directly or indirectly—any limitation, specification, or discrimination as to sex shall be unlawful unless based upon a bona fide occupational qualification.

Fringe Benefits

It is an unlawful employment practice under Title VII for an employer to discriminate between men and women with regard to fringe benefits. Fringe benefits may include medical, hospital, accident, life insurance and retirement benefits; profit-sharing and bonus plans; leave; and other terms, conditions, and privileges of employment.

The EEOC has determined that where an employer conditions benefits available to employees and their spouses and families on whether the employee is the "head of the household" or "principal wage earner" in the family, the benefits tend to be available only to male employees and their families. Due to the fact that such conditions discriminatorily affect the rights of women employees, and that "head of household" or "principal wage earner" status bears no relationship to job performance, benefits which are so conditioned will be found a prima facie violation of the prohibitions against sex discrimination under Title VII.

It is also an unlawful employment practice for an employer to have a pension or retirement plan which establishes different optional or compulsory retirement ages based on sex, or which differentiates in benefits on the basis of sex.

Further, it is an unlawful employment practice for an employer to:

1. Make benefits available for the wives and families of male employees where the same benefits are not made available for the husbands and families of female employees; or

2. Make benefits available for the wives of male employees which are not made available for female employees; or

3. Make benefits available to the husbands of female employees that are not made available for male employees.

An example of such an unlawful employment practice is a situation in which wives of male employees receive maternity benefits while female employees receive no such benefits.

Further, it is not a defense under Title VII to a charge of sex discrimination in benefits that the cost of such benefits is greater with respect to one sex than the other.

Statistics

In 2006, the EEOC received 23,247 charges of sex-based discrimination. The EEOC resolved 23,364 sex discrimination charges in 2006 and recovered $99.1 million in monetary benefits for charging parties and other aggrieved individuals, not including monetary benefits obtained through litigation.

A table of sex-based discrimination charges and resolutions (2000–2006) is set forth in Appendix 14.

SEXUAL HARASSMENT

In 1980, the EEOC stated that sexual harassment was a form of gender discrimination that is prohibited under Title VII. The EEOC then issued regulations defining illegal sexual harassment. In 1986, the U.S. Supreme Court also held that sexual harassment was a form of illegal employment discrimination. An individual is permitted to bring a claim for sexual harassment under Title VII.

Equal Employment Opportunity Commission Standards

The EEOC basically defines sexual harassment as "unwelcome" sexual advances, requests for sexual favors and other verbal or physical conduct of a sexual nature when:

1. Submission to such conduct is made either explicitly or implicitly a term or condition of an individual's employment;

2. Submission to or rejection of such conduct by an individual is used as the basis for employment decisions affecting such individual; or

3. Such conduct has the purpose or effect of unreasonably interfering with an individual's work performance or creating an intimidating, hostile or offensive working environment.

Further, in 1988, the EEOC amended its guidelines to extend legal responsibility on employers for the sexual harassment of employees by non-employees. It holds an employer responsible for the acts of non-employees when the employer, or its agents or supervisory employees, knows or should have known of the conduct and fails to take appropriate corrective action.

When investigating allegations of sexual harassment, the EEOC looks at the whole record: the circumstances, such as the nature of the sexual advances, and the context in which the alleged incidents occurred. A determination on the allegations is made from the facts on a case-by-case basis.

Standard of Conduct

There are three major standards that are examined to determine whether behavior constitutes illegal sexual harassment, as further discussed below.

The Reasonable Female Employee Standard

The standard a court usually uses in determining whether conduct violates the law is whether or not a "reasonable" female employee would find the conduct offensive. In addition, the individual can set the boundaries of "reasonableness" for herself by communicating to the offender that she finds his behavior offensive. If he thereafter persists, he will have violated the standard of conduct she set.

Of course, to prevail in a lawsuit, there must be some proof that the communication took place, e.g. a letter to the offender and the employer, and proof that the offensive behavior persisted after the offender was notified.

The Severe and Pervasive Standard

Another factor a court uses to determine whether certain conduct constitutes sexual harassment is whether the behavior was so severe or pervasive that it created a hostile work environment. According to the EEOC, some factors which indicate that behavior was "severe and pervasive" include:

1. The type of behavior, e.g. whether it was verbal, physical or both;
2. The frequency of the behavior;
3. The position of the offender, e.g. supervisor or co-worker;
4. The number of individuals who engaged in such behaviors; and
5. Whether the behavior was directed at one or more individuals.

Of course, certain types of behavior do not have to be cumulative, but need only occur once to be deemed illegal, e.g. employment or promotions that are conditioned on sexual favors, or outright sexual attacks.

The Unwelcome Conduct Standard

Although it may appear that any behavior which gives rise to a complaint would qualify as "unwelcome," the court may examine additional criteria to make its determination, such as whether the behavior was unwelcome at the time it occurred.

For example, a female employee may have engaged in sexual behavior with another voluntarily at one time. However, if thereafter she has communicated her desire not to continue in such a relationship, any subsequent sexual demands placed upon her would be deemed "unwelcome" and would likely constitute illegal sexual harassment.

In addition, even if the woman "voluntarily" goes along with the offensive behavior, if she does so out of fear of losing her job, this would also constitute "unwelcome" behavior.

The Sexually Offensive Atmosphere

Courts have recognized that creating a sexually offensive atmosphere—e.g. by displaying pornographic materials in the workplace, or by engaging in vulgar and lewd behavior—is a violation of sexual harassment laws. This is so even if the offensive conduct is not directed at any particular individual. The concern is that the creation of such a sexually offensive atmosphere demeans, and works to the disadvantage of, the female employees.

The Hostile Work Environment

Creation of a hostile work environment usually involves intimidation tactics used to try and force women out of a traditionally all-male industry. Even if there is no sexual misconduct, the courts have still found there to be a sexual harassment violation. The courts will look at whether the offensive behavior would have been directed at a male employee.

Statistics

In 2006, EEOC received 12,025 charges of sexual harassment. 15.4% of those charges were filed by males. The EEOC resolved 11,936 sexual harassment charges in 2006, and recovered $48.8 million in monetary benefits for charging parties and other aggrieved individuals, not including monetary benefits obtained through litigation.

A table of sexual harassment charges and resolutions (2000–2006) is set forth in Appendix 15.

PREGNANCY DISCRIMINATION

The Pregnancy Discrimination Act of 1978 is an amendment to Title VII. Discrimination on the basis of pregnancy, childbirth or a related medical condition constitutes unlawful sex discrimination under Title VII. Women affected by pregnancy or related conditions must be treated in the same manner as other applicants or employees with similar abilities or limitations. A written or unwritten employment policy or practice that excludes from employment applicants or employees because of pregnancy, childbirth or related medical conditions is in prima facie violation of Title VII.

An employer cannot refuse to hire a woman because of her pregnancy-related condition as long as she is able to perform the major functions of her job. An employer cannot refuse to hire her because of its prejudices against pregnant workers or the prejudices of co-workers, clients or customers.

In addition, an employer may not single out pregnancy-related conditions for special procedures to determine an employee's ability to work. However, an employer may use any procedure used to screen other employees' ability to work.

For example, if an employer requires its employees to submit a doctor's statement concerning their inability to work before granting leave or paying sick benefits, the employer may require employees affected by pregnancy-related conditions to submit such statements in order to qualify for maternity leave.

If an employee is temporarily unable to perform her job due to pregnancy, the employer must treat her the same as any other temporarily disabled employee; for example, by providing modified tasks, alternative assignments, disability leave or leave without pay.

Pregnant employees must be permitted to work as long as they are able to perform their jobs. If an employee has been absent from work as a result of a pregnancy-related condition and recovers, her employer may not require her to remain on leave until the baby's birth. In addition, an employer may not have a rule that prohibits an employee from returning to work for a predetermined length of time after childbirth. Employers must hold open a job for a pregnancy-related absence the same length of time that jobs are held open for employees on sick or disability leave.

Health Insurance

Any health insurance provided by an employer must cover expenses for pregnancy-related conditions on the same basis as costs for other medical conditions. However, health insurance for expenses arising from abortion is not required, except where the life of the mother is endangered.

Pregnancy-related expenses should be reimbursed exactly as those incurred for other medical conditions, whether payment is on a fixed basis or a percentage of reasonable and customary charge basis. The amounts payable by the insurance provider can be limited only to the same extent as costs for other conditions. No additional, increased or larger deductible can be imposed.

If a health insurance plan excludes benefit payments for pre-existing conditions when the insured's coverage becomes effective, benefits can be denied for medical costs arising from an existing pregnancy. Further, employers must provide the same level of health benefits for spouses of male employees as they do for spouses of female employees.

Fringe Benefits

Pregnancy related benefits cannot be limited to married employees. In an all-female workforce or job classification, benefits must be provided for pregnancy-related conditions if benefits are provided for other medical conditions.

If an employer provides any benefits to workers on leave, the employer must provide the same benefits for those on leave for pregnancy-related conditions. Employees with pregnancy-related disabilities must be treated the same as other temporarily disabled employees for accrual and crediting of seniority, vacation calculation, pay increases and temporary disability benefits.

Statistics

In 2006, EEOC received 4,901 charges of pregnancy-based discrimination. The EEOC resolved 4,629 pregnancy discrimination charges in 2006, and recovered $10.4 million in monetary benefits for charging parties and other aggrieved individuals, not including monetary benefits obtained through litigation.

A table of pregnancy-based discrimination charges and resolutions (2000–2006) is set forth in Appendix 16.

THE EQUAL PAY ACT OF 1963

The Equal Pay Act, an amendment to the Fair Labor Standards Act, provides that equal pay must be paid to workers for equal work, regardless of gender, if the jobs they perform require "equal skill, effort, and responsibility and are performed under similar working conditions in the same establishment." Each of these factors is summarized below:

Skill

Skill is measured by factors such as the experience, ability, education, and training required to perform the job. The key issue is what skills are required for the job, not what skills the individual employees may have.

Effort

Effort refers to the amount of physical or mental exertion needed to perform the job.

Responsibility

Responsibility is the degree of accountability required in performing the job.

Working Conditions

Working conditions encompass two factors:

1. The physical surroundings like temperature, fumes, and ventilation; and
2. Hazards

Establishment

The prohibition against compensation discrimination under the EPA applies only to jobs within any establishment. An establishment is a distinct physical place of business rather than an entire business or enterprise consisting of several places of business. However, in some circumstances, physically separate places of business should be treated as one establishment. For example, if a central administrative unit hires employees, sets their compensation, and assigns them to work locations, the separate work sites can be considered part of one establishment.

Covered Employers

The EPA covers all employers who are covered by the Fair Labor Standards Act (FLSA). Thus, virtually all private employers are subject to the provisions of the EPA, which covers both current employees and job applicants. Although discrimination in pay based on sex is also prohibited by Title VII, the EPA serves to cover employers who may not be subject to Title VII due to the size of the company.

Affirmative Defenses

Pay differentials are permitted when they are based on seniority, merit, quantity or quality of production, or a factor other than sex. These are known as "affirmative defenses" and it is the employer's burden to prove that they apply.

In correcting a pay differential, no employee's pay may be reduced. Instead, the pay of the lower paid employee must be increased.

Statistics

In 2006, the EEOC received 861 charges of equal pay act violations. The EEOC resolved 748 equal pay act charges in 2006 and recovered $3.1 million in monetary benefits for charging parties and other aggrieved individuals, not including monetary benefits obtained through litigation.

A table of Equal Pay Act charges and resolutions (2000–2006) is set forth in Appendix 17.

CHAPTER 7: DISCRIMINATION ON THE BASIS OF NATIONAL ORIGIN

IN GENERAL

Title VII of the Civil Rights Act of 1964 protects individuals against employment discrimination on the basis of national origin, making it unlawful to discriminate against any employee or applicant because of the individual's national origin, in regard to hiring, termination, promotion, compensation, job training, or any other term, condition, or privilege of employment.

Under Title VII, no person can be denied equal employment opportunity because of birthplace, ancestry, culture, or linguistic characteristics common to a specific ethnic group. In addition, equal employment opportunity cannot be denied because of:

1. Marriage to, or association with, persons of a national origin group;
2. Membership in, or association with, specific ethnic promotion groups;
3. Attendance or participation in schools, churches, temples or mosques generally associated with a national origin group; or
4. A surname associated with a national origin group.

In examining charges based on unlawful national origin discrimination, the EEOC will apply general Title VII principles, such as disparate treatment and adverse impact.

ENGLISH-ONLY RULE

A rule requiring employees to speak only English at all times on the job may violate Title VII, unless an employer shows it is necessary for conducting business. If an employer believes the English-only rule is critical for business purposes, employees have to be told when they must speak English and the consequences for violating the rule.

The primary language of an individual is often an essential national origin characteristic. Prohibiting employees at all times, in the workplace, from speaking their primary language or the language they speak most comfortably, disadvantages an individual's employment opportunities on the basis of national origin. It may also create an atmosphere of inferiority, isolation and intimidation based on national origin that could result in a discriminatory working environment.

Therefore, the EEOC presumes that such a rule violates Title VII and will closely scrutinize its application. In addition, any negative employment decision based on breaking an English-only rule will be considered evidence of discrimination if the employer did not tell employees of the rule.

DENIAL OF EMPLOYMENT BASED ON ACCENT

An employer must show a legitimate nondiscriminatory reason for the denial of employment opportunity because of an individual's accent or manner of speaking. EEOC investigations will focus on the qualifications of the person and whether his or her accent or manner of speaking had a detrimental effect on job performance.

Requiring employees or applicants to be fluent in English may violate Title VII if the rule is adopted to exclude individuals of a particular national origin and is not related to job performance.

HARASSMENT

Harassment on the basis of national origin is a violation of Title VII. An ethnic slur or other verbal or physical conduct because of an individual's nationality constitutes harassment if it creates an intimidating, hostile or offensive working environment, unreasonably interferes with work performance or negatively affects an individual's employment opportunities.

Employers have a responsibility to maintain a workplace free of national origin harassment. Employers may be responsible for any on-the-job harassment by their agents and supervisory employees, regardless of whether the acts were authorized or specifically forbidden by the employer. Under certain circumstances, an employer may be responsible for the acts of non-employees who harass their employees at work.

DISCRIMINATORY IMMIGRATION-RELATED PRACTICES

The Immigration Reform and Control Act of 1986 (IRCA) requires employers to prove all employees hired after November 6, 1986, are legally authorized to work in the United States. IRCA also prohibits discrimination based on national origin or citizenship.

An employer who singles out individuals of a particular national origin, or individuals who appear to be foreign, to provide employment verification may have violated both IRCA and Title VII. Employers who impose citizenship requirements or give preference to U.S. citizens in hiring or employment opportunities may have violated IRCA, unless there are legal or contractual requirements for particular jobs. Employers also may have violated Title VII if a requirement or preference has the purpose or effect of discriminating against individuals of a particular national origin.

THE NATIONAL SECURITY EXCEPTION

It is not an unlawful employment practice to deny employment opportunities to any individual who does not fulfill the national security requirements. The head of a Federal agency or department is authorized to suspend or remove an employee on grounds of national security.

THE BONA FIDE OCCUPATIONAL QUALIFICATION EXCEPTION

Under the bona fide occupational qualification exception of Title VII, national origin may be a bona fide occupational qualification. However, that exception shall be strictly construed.

CITIZENSHIP REQUIREMENTS

In those circumstances, where citizenship requirements have the purpose or effect of discriminating against an individual on the basis of national origin, they are prohibited by Title VII. For example, some state laws prohibit the employment of non-citizens. Where these laws are in conflict with Title VII, they are superseded under Title VII.

EMPLOYER SELECTION PROCEDURES

In investigating an employer's selection procedures for adverse impact on the basis of national origin, the EEOC will apply the Uniform Guidelines on Employee Selection Procedures (UGESP), 29 CFR Part 1607. Employers should refer to the UGESP for guidance on matters, such as adverse impact, validation and recordkeeping requirements for national origin groups.

For example, because height or weight requirements tend to exclude individuals on the basis of national origin, an employer is expected to evaluate these selection procedures for adverse impact, regardless of whether the total selection process has an adverse impact based on national origin.

The EEOC has found that the use of the following selection procedures may be discriminatory on the basis of national origin and, therefore, will carefully investigate charges involving these selection procedures for both disparate treatment and adverse impact on the basis of national origin:

1. Fluency-in-English requirements, such as denying employment opportunities because of an individual's foreign accent or inability to communicate well in English.

2. Training or education requirements which deny employment opportunities to an individual because of his or her foreign training or education, or which require an individual to be foreign trained or educated.

STATISTICS

In 2006, the EEOC received 8,327 charges of national origin discrimination. The EEOC resolved 8,181 charges in 2006, and monetary benefits for charging parties totaled $21.2 million, not including monetary benefits obtained through litigation.

A table of national origin-based discrimination charges and resolutions (2000–2006), is set forth in Appendix 18.

CHAPTER 8: DISCRIMINATION ON THE BASIS OF AGE

IN GENERAL

As the baby boomer generation reaches their fifties and sixties, the American workforce is comprised of a much larger population of older employees. Many of these employees have been working for a long period of time. Thus, they are generally compensated at a much higher rate than their younger counterparts, resulting in quite an expense for the employer. This creates an economic incentive for the employer to lay off the older workers. Once unemployed, the older worker has a much more difficult time finding new employment.

Fortunately, there is legislation in place that affords some protection to older workers who face age discrimination in employment. An individual, age 40 years or older, is protected under the Age Discrimination in Employment Act (ADEA), if he or she is fired or laid off because of age.

Under the ADEA, it is unlawful to discriminate against a person because of his or her age with respect to any term, condition, or privilege of employment, including hiring, firing, promotion, layoff, compensation, benefits, job assignments, and training.

It is also unlawful to retaliate against an individual for opposing employment practices that discriminate based on age, or for filing an age discrimination charge, testifying, or participating in any way in an investigation, proceeding, or litigation under the ADEA.

COVERED EMPLOYERS

The ADEA applies to employers with 20 or more employees, including state and local governments. It also applies to employment agencies and labor organizations, as well as to the federal government.

ADEA PROTECTIONS

ADEA protections include the following:

Apprenticeship Programs

It is generally unlawful for apprenticeship programs, including joint labor-management apprenticeship programs, to discriminate on the basis of an individual's age. Age limitations in apprenticeship programs are valid only if they fall within certain specific exceptions under the ADEA or if the EEOC grants a specific exemption.

Job Notices and Advertisements

The ADEA generally makes it unlawful to include age preferences, limitations, or specifications in job notices or advertisements. A job notice or advertisement may specify an age limit only in the rare circumstances where age is shown to be a "bona fide occupational qualification" (BFOQ) reasonably necessary to the normal operation of the business.

Pre-Employment Inquiries

The ADEA does not specifically prohibit an employer from asking an applicant's age or date of birth. However, because such inquiries may deter older workers from applying for employment or may otherwise indicate possible intent to discriminate based on age, requests for age information will be closely scrutinized to make sure that the inquiry was made for a lawful purpose, rather than for a purpose prohibited by the ADEA.

Benefits

The Older Workers Benefit Protection Act of 1990 (OWBPA) amended the ADEA, to specifically prohibit employers from denying benefits to older employees. Congress recognized that the cost of providing certain benefits to older workers is greater than the cost of providing those same benefits to younger workers, and that those greater costs would create a disincentive to hire older workers.

Therefore, in limited circumstances, an employer may be permitted to reduce benefits based on age, as long as the cost of providing the reduced benefits to older workers is the same as the cost of providing benefits to younger workers.

In addition, some employers attempt to lay off older workers just prior to the vesting of their pension plans. Under the OWBPA, it is illegal for an employer to:

1. Use an employee's age as the basis for discrimination in benefits; and
2. Target older workers for staff cutting. Such actions would also violate the ADEA, as discussed above.

EXCEPTIONS TO COVERAGE

The ADEA does not apply in the following situations:

1. Mandatory retirement at age 65 of executives or people in high policy-making positions is permitted if the retired employee would receive annual pension benefits worth $44,000 or more.

2. Certain employees of police and fire departments, tenured university faculty, and certain federal employees engaged in enforcement and air traffic control positions, may be exempt from coverage under the ADEA.

3. If age is an essential part of one's job—i.e., it is a bona fide occupational qualification related to performance abilities—the employee might be exempt from coverage under the ADEA.

Nevertheless, remedies may be available under state anti-discrimination laws, which may apply in situations where the ADEA does not apply, e.g. in the case of private employers of less than 20 employees. In fact, many of the state laws provide more comprehensive coverage than the ADEA. Therefore, the reader is advised to check the law of his or her own jurisdiction concerning protection afforded under the state anti-discrimination statutes.

WAIVER OF ADEA RIGHTS

An employer may ask an employee to waive his or her rights or claims under the ADEA, either in the settlement of an ADEA administrative or court claim, or in connection with an exit incentive program or other employment termination program.

The ADEA contains specific minimum standards that must be met in order for a waiver to be considered knowing and voluntary and, therefore, valid. Among other requirements, a valid ADEA waiver must comply with the following:

1. The waiver must be in writing and be understandable;

2. The waiver must specifically refer to ADEA rights or claims;

3. The waiver must not waive rights or claims that may arise in the future;

4. The waiver must be in exchange for valuable consideration;

5. The waiver must advise the individual in writing to consult an attorney before signing the waiver; and

6. The waiver must provide the individual at least twenty-one (21) days to consider the agreement and at least seven (7) days to revoke the agreement after signing it.

If an employer requests an ADEA waiver in connection with an exit incentive program or other employment termination program, the minimum requirements for a valid waiver are more extensive.

BURDEN OF PROOF IN AN ADEA CASE

In order to prevail in an age discrimination lawsuit, the employee has the burden of proving a prima facie case, which includes a showing that:

1. The employee is a member of the protected class, i.e. over 40;
2. The employee is adversely affected by the employer's action; and
3. Age was the determining factor in the employer's action.

Once a prima facie case has been demonstrated, the employer has the burden of showing that the action was taken for some legitimate nondiscriminatory reason. If the employer is able to do so, the burden shifts again to the employee to show that the stated reason is merely a pretext. If the employee prevails, he or she may be entitled to a money damage award, and equitable relief, e.g. reinstatement.

STATISTICS

In 2006, the EEOC received 16,548 charges of age discrimination. The EEOC resolved 14,146 age discrimination charges in 2006, and recovered $51.5 million in monetary benefits for charging parties and other aggrieved individuals, not including monetary benefits obtained through litigation.

A table of age-based discrimination charges and resolutions (2000–2006) is set forth in Appendix 19.

CHAPTER 9: DISCRIMINATION ON THE BASIS OF DISABILITY

IN GENERAL

Title I of the Americans with Disabilities Act (ADA) addresses the rights of individuals with disabilities in employment settings. According to the U.S. Department of Justice, the purpose of Title I is to ensure that qualified individuals with disabilities are protected from discrimination on the basis of disability. As long as the individual is qualified for an employment opportunity, that person cannot be denied that opportunity simply because he or she has a disability, and must therefore be given the same consideration for employment that individuals without disabilities are given.

COVERED EMPLOYERS

The Title I employment provisions apply to private employers, state and local governments, employment agencies, educational institutions, and labor unions. Employers with 25 or more employees were covered as of July 26, 1992. Employers with 15 or more employees were covered two years later, beginning July 26, 1994.

PROHIBITED PRACTICES

The ADA prohibits discrimination in all employment practices, including job application procedures, hiring, firing, advancement, compensation, training, and other terms, conditions, and privileges of employment. It applies to recruitment, advertising, tenure, layoff, leave, fringe benefits, and all other employment-related activities.

COVERED PERSONS

Employment discrimination is prohibited against "qualified individuals with disabilities." This includes applicants for employment and employees.

Disability Defined

An individual with disabilities is defined as:

1. A person who has a physical or mental impairment that substantially limits one or more major life activities;

2. A person who has a record of such an impairment; or

3. A person who is regarded as having such an impairment.

Under the first part of the definition, the person must have an impairment that must substantially limit his or her major life activities such as seeing, hearing, speaking, walking, breathing, performing manual tasks, learning, caring for oneself, and working.

Thus, an individual with epilepsy, paralysis, HIV infection, AIDS, a substantial hearing or visual impairment, mental retardation, or a specific learning disability is covered, but an individual with a minor, non-chronic condition of short duration, such as a sprain, broken limb, or the flu, generally would not be covered.

For example, an employee suffers a broken wrist that is expected to heal, but while it is healing he is unable to perform the essential functions of his job as an assembly-line worker. This employee is not protected by the ADA because, although he is "impaired," the impairment does not substantially limit a major life activity because it is of limited duration and will have no long-term effect.

Under the second part of the definition, an individual with a "record" of a disability would cover a person who has recovered from an impairment that substantially limited his or her major life activities, such as cancer or mental illness.

Under the third part of the definition, individuals who are regarded as having a substantially limiting impairment, even though they may not have such an impairment, are protected. For example, this provision would protect a qualified individual with a severe facial disfigurement from being denied employment because an employer feared the "negative reactions" of customers or co-workers.

In addition, employees who are discriminated against because they know, are associated with, or are related to a disabled individual are also protected from adverse action caused by bias or ignorance concerning certain disabilities. For example, if an employee's family member suffers from a disease, such as AIDS, he or she should not suffer job discrimination due to the ignorant assumption that AIDS can be transmitted through casual contact.

Qualified Individual

To be covered by the ADA, the disabled person must be "qualified"—i.e., he or she must meet the legitimate experience, education, or other requirements of the position he or she holds or is applying for, and must be able to perform the "essential functions" of the position, with or without "reasonable accommodations." This includes applicants for employment as well as employees.

Essential Functions

The law requires that the disabled individual must be able to perform the "essential functions" of the job. The term "essential" was used so that individuals would not be deemed unqualified merely because they are unable to perform incidental or inconsequential tasks related to the position.

Essential functions are the basic tasks that an employee must be able to perform, with or without reasonable accommodation. Prior to advertising for an open position, an employer should carefully examine each job description to determine which functions or tasks are essential to performance.

The essential functions of a particular job may depend on an evaluation of the following factors:

1. Whether the existence of the position is for the purposes of performing the function;

2. The degree of expertise or skill required to perform the particular function; and

3. The number of other employees available to perform the function or assist in performing the function.

If a complaint is brought and the EEOC investigates, a written job description which carefully describes the essential functions of the position, and which was prepared prior to advertising for the position, will weigh in the employer's favor.

REASONABLE ACCOMMODATIONS

If an individual is qualified to perform the essential job functions, except for certain limitations caused by their disability, the employer is obliged to consider whether the individual could perform these functions if "reasonable accommodations" are provided.

The guidelines promulgated by the EEOC provide that an employer must make a reasonable effort to provide an appropriate reasonable accommodation for a qualified disabled employee who requests one. A reasonable accommodation is any modification or adjustment to the work environment that will enable a qualified disabled individual to perform the essential job functions.

A reasonable accommodation must also be made to enable a disabled individual to participate in the job application process, and to enjoy the benefits and privileges of employment equal to those available to other employees.

Reasonable accommodations may include:

1. Acquiring or modifying equipment or devices;
2. Job restructuring;
3. Providing part-time or modified work schedules;
4. Adjusting or modifying examinations, training materials or policies; and
5. Providing readers and interpreters.

If the employee is unable to perform the "essential functions" of his or her position—and there are no reasonable accommodations that would enable the employee to function in that position—a reasonable accommodation may include reassignment to another available position.

However, an employer is not required to find a disabled employee alternative employment if it is not reasonably available. In that case, the disabled employee would not be "qualified" because he or she does not meet the requirements of the position, and is unable to perform the essential functions of the position, with or without a reasonable accommodation. In addition, if an employee refuses to accept an offered accommodation, the individual may likewise be considered not "qualified."

As discussed below, a reasonable accommodation may also include making the workplace readily accessible to and usable by disabled persons. For example, it would be a "reasonable accommodation" for an employer to permit a wheelchair bound employee to adjust his or her work hours so that they he or she is not traveling during rush hour.

Disclosure

Because an employer is only required to accommodate a "known" disability of a qualified applicant or employee, the employee must disclose that he or she has a disability which is covered under the statute, and requires a "reasonable accommodation."

Undue Hardship

Despite the requirement to provide reasonable accommodations, an employer is not required to provide a reasonable accommodation that would pose an "undue hardship" on the business.

An undue hardship is defined as an "action requiring significant difficulty or expense" when considered in light of a number of factors, such as the cost of the accommodation in relation to the resources of the employer, or whether the accommodation would fundamentally alter the nature or operation of the business. A large employer with greater resources would be expected to make more extensive accommodations than would be required of a smaller employer.

If a particular accommodation would be an undue hardship, the employer must try to identify another accommodation that would not pose such a hardship. If the cost of the accommodation is prohibitive, the following alternatives may be considered:

1. Whether there is funding available from an outside source, such as a vocational rehabilitation agency;
2. Whether the cost of providing the accommodation can be offset by state or federal tax credits or deductions; or
3. Whether the applicant or employee will provide the accommodation, or is willing to contribute towards the cost.

Direct Threat

An employer does not have to hire an individual who poses a "direct threat" to his or her health or safety, or the health and safety of others, if the risk cannot be eliminated or significantly reduced by means of a reasonable accommodation.

A direct threat is defined as one that carries with it a significant risk of substantial harm, not a slightly increased risk or a speculative or remote risk. If the employer claims that a direct threat exists, he or she must substantiate that the risk is real and not merely a perceived threat.

Such proof may include objective medical evidence that there is a significant risk that substantial harm could occur in the workplace.

For example, transmission of AIDS/HIV disease will rarely be a legitimate "direct threat" because it has been medically established that the illness cannot be transmitted by casual contact. AIDS/HIV disease can only be transmitted by sexual contact with an infected individual, exposure to infected blood or blood products, or perinatally from an infected mother to her infant during pregnancy, birth or breastfeeding. Thus, there is little possibility the illness could ever be transmitted in a workplace setting.

ACCESSIBILITY

The employer's obligation under Title I is to provide access for an individual applicant to participate in the job application process, and for an individual employee with a disability to perform the essential functions of his/her job, including access to a building, to the work site, to needed equipment, and to all facilities used by employees.

For example, if an employee lounge is located in a place inaccessible to an employee using a wheelchair, the lounge might be modified or relocated, or comparable facilities might be provided in a location that would enable the individual to take a break with co-workers. The employer must provide such access unless it would cause an undue hardship.

Under Title I, an employer is not required to make its existing facilities accessible until a particular applicant or employee with a particular disability needs an accommodation, and then the modifications should meet that individual's work needs. However, employers should consider initiating changes that will provide general accessibility, particularly for job applicants, since it is likely that people with disabilities will be applying for jobs.

PREFERENTIAL TREATMENT

The law does not require the employer to give the disabled applicant or employee any preferential treatment over other applicants or employees. Employers are free to select the most qualified individual available provided those decisions are based on reasons unrelated to the disability.

For example, suppose two persons apply for a job as a typist and an essential function of the job is to type 75 words per minute accurately. One applicant, an individual with a disability, who is provided with a reasonable accommodation for a typing test, types 50 words per minute; the other applicant who has no disability accurately types 75 words per minute.

The employer can hire the applicant with the higher typing speed, if typing speed is needed for successful performance of the job.

TAX CREDITS AND DEDUCTIONS

A special tax credit is available to help smaller employers make accommodations required by the ADA. An eligible small business may take a tax credit of up to $5,000 per year for accommodations made to comply with the ADA. The credit is available for one-half the cost of "eligible access expenditures" that are more than $250 but less than $10,250.

A full tax deduction, up to $15,000 per year, is also available to any business for expenses of removing qualified architectural or transportation barriers. Expenses covered include costs of removing barriers created by steps, narrow doors, inaccessible parking spaces, restroom facilities, and transportation vehicles.

RECORDKEEPING REQUIREMENT

The ADA requires an employer to maintain records, including: (i) job application forms; (ii) all records related to hiring; (iii) requests for reasonable accommodations, (iv) promotion, demotion, transfer, lay-off or termination records; (v) compensation schedules; and (vi) training or apprenticeship selection records.

Records are to be maintained for a period of one year after either: (i) the record is made; or (ii) the particular action is taken, whichever occurs later. However, if a charge of discrimination is filed or an action is brought by the EEOC, an employer must save all personnel records related to the charge until its final disposition.

NOTICE REQUIREMENT

The ADA requires employers to post a notice describing the ADA and its provisions, in an accessible format, available to all applicants, employees and members of labor organizations. The EEOC provides posters summarizing these and other Federal legal requirements for nondiscrimination. The EEOC also provides guidance to employers on making this information available in accessible formats for people who have disabilities preventing them from reading the notice, such as sight-impaired individuals.

MEDICAL EXAMINATIONS

Under Title I, an employer cannot require a job applicant to submit to a medical examination prior to making a job offer. An employer is also prohibited from asking the applicant about the existence, nature or severity of a disability, although an applicant may be questioned about his or her ability to perform specific job functions.

Nevertheless, a job offer may be conditioned on the results of a medical examination if the examination is required for all prospective employees in similar jobs.

Employment may thus be conditioned upon a satisfactory medical examination once the job offer is made. Nevertheless, if the results of the medical examination reveal a disability, the employer must still hire the individual unless the disability is employment-related, and no reasonable accommodations are available that would enable the applicant to perform the essential functions of the position.

Once an applicant is hired, an employer cannot require a medical examination, or ask the employee about his or her disability, unless it can be shown that these requirements are job related and necessary for the conduct of the business. Nevertheless, an employer may conduct voluntary medical examinations under an employee health program.

The results of any medical examinations, or other information gathered concerning an employee's disability, must be kept confidential, and maintained in a separate medical file.

Drug and Alcohol Addiction

The prohibition against pre-job offer medical examinations does not apply to testing for illegal drug use. An employee or applicant who "currently" uses illegal drugs is excluded from the definition of a "qualified" individual with a disability, and, thus, not protected by the ADA.

However, the ADA does not exclude (i) individuals who have successfully completed a drug rehabilitation program—or who are currently in such a program—and are no longer illegally using drugs; and (ii) individuals erroneously regarded as engaging in the illegal use of drugs.

An individual suffering from alcoholism is considered a person with a disability protected by the ADA, even if currently consuming alcohol, provided he or she is qualified to perform the essential functions of the job. Nevertheless, the employer is free to fire or otherwise discipline an alcoholic employee if their addiction adversely affects their job performance or conduct. The employer can further require that the alcoholic employee refrain from drinking alcohol while on the job.

STATISTICS

In 2006, the EEOC received 15,575 charges of disability discrimination. The EEOC resolved 15,045 disability discrimination charges in 2006, and recovered $48.8 million in monetary benefits for charging parties and other aggrieved individuals, not including monetary benefits obtained through litigation.

A table of Americans with Disabilities Act (ADA) charges and resolutions (2000–2006) is set forth in Appendix 20.

CHAPTER 10: ADDITIONAL BASIS OF DISCRIMINATION

IN GENERAL

The U.S. Equal Employment Opportunity Commission (EEOC) does not enforce the protections that prohibit discrimination and harassment based on sexual orientation, status as a parent, marital status and political affiliation. However, other federal agencies and many states and municipalities do offer this protection. You should contact your local civil rights agency for more information.

FEDERAL PROTECTION

The Civil Service Reform Act of 1978 (CSRA)

The Civil Service Reform Act of 1978 (CSRA), as amended, prohibits federal employees who have authority to take, direct others to take, recommend or approve any personnel action from discriminating against applicants and employees on the basis of race, color, sex, religion, national origin, age, disability, marital status or political affiliation, and from discriminating against an applicant or employee on the basis of conduct which does not adversely affect the performance of the applicant or employee. The Office of Personnel Management (OPM) has interpreted the prohibition of discrimination based on "conduct" to include discrimination based on sexual orientation.

The Office of Special Counsel (OSC) and the Merit Systems Protection Board (MSPB) enforce the prohibitions against federal employment discrimination codified in the CSRA, but will defer those basis of discrimination that fall under the EEOC's jurisdiction to the respective federal agency and its EEO process.

Executive Order 13087 - Sexual Orientation Discrimination

Executive Order 13087 issued on May 28, 1998, prohibits discrimination based upon sexual orientation within Executive Branch civilian employment. Executive Order 13087 amended Executive Order 11478.

This Executive Order added sexual orientation to the list of categories for which discrimination is prohibited. Many Cabinet level agencies have also issued policy statements prohibiting discrimination based on sexual orientation.

Executive Order 13152 - Status as a Parent

Executive Order 13152 further amended Executive Order 11478 on May 2, 2000, to provide for a uniform policy for the federal government to prohibit discrimination based on an individual's status as a parent.

Executive Order 13152 states that "status as a parent" refers to the status of an individual who, with respect to an individual who is under the age of 18 or who is 18 or older but is incapable of self-care because of a physical or mental disability, is:

1. A biological parent;
2. An adoptive parent;
3. A foster parent;
4. A stepparent;
5. A custodian of a legal ward;
6. A person in loco parentis over such an individual; or
7. A person actively seeking legal custody or adoption of such an individual.

Executive Order 11478

As a result of the above amendments, Section 1 of Executive Order 11478 now reads as follows:

> It is the policy of the government of the United States to provide equal opportunity in federal employment for all persons, to prohibit discrimination in employment because of race, color, religion, sex, national origin, handicap, age, sexual orientation or status as a parent, and to promote the full realization of equal employment opportunity through a continuing affirmative program in each executive department and agency. This policy of equal opportunity applies to and must be an integral part of every aspect of personnel policy and practice in the employment, development, advancement, and treatment of civilian employees of the federal government, to the extent permitted by law.

Filing a Discrimination Complaint

The Civil Service Reform Act handles discrimination complaints based on sexual orientation or status as a parent, Executive Order 13087, and Executive Order 13152. In addition, some federal agencies have developed parallel EEO complaint procedures allowing employees to file EEO complaints based on sexual orientation within their agencies.

Federal employees should check with their agencies to see if procedures exist to handle these complaints. In addition, employees should check their respective collective bargaining agreements and their agencies negotiated grievance procedures to determine whether there are any grievance procedures that address these issues.

STATE AND LOCAL LAWS

Seventeen states and the District of Columbia currently prohibit sexual orientation employment discrimination by private employers. Those states include: California. Connecticut, Hawaii, Illinois, Maine, Maryland, Massachusetts, Minnesota, Nevada, New Hampshire, New Jersey, New Mexico, New York, Rhode Island, Vermont, Washington, and Wisconsin. Some of these states also specifically prohibit discrimination based on gender identity.

Private employers who operate their business in these states, or in any county or city that prohibits sexual orientation discrimination, must follow the law despite the fact that there is no governing federal law.

In addition, six states have laws prohibiting sexual orientation discrimination in public workplaces only: Colorado, Delaware, Indiana, Michigan, Montana, and Pennsylvania.

Locally, more than 180 cities and counties nationwide prohibit sexual orientation discrimination in at least some workplaces.

To find out whether your state, county, or city has a law prohibiting discrimination on the basis of sexual orientation, contact your state labor department or your state fair employment office.

California Statute

California's statute prohibiting sexual orientation discrimination in the workplace is an example of a typical state law. Under California law, it is illegal for an employer to discriminate against an employee because of that employee's sexual orientation or perceived sexual orientation.

Perceived Sexual Orientation

It is illegal in California for an employer to discriminate against an employee on the basis of that employee's *perceived* sexual orientation. Thus, if an employer believes an employee is a homosexual, and fires him because of that, it is illegal whether or not the employee is actually a homosexual.

Statute of Limitations

Under the California law, the employee must make a complaint to the California Labor Commission no more than 30 days after he or she is discriminated against. Only after the Labor Commission has processed the claim may the employee sue in court.

Relationship to Other Laws

Frequently the same actions that violate the laws against sexual orientation discrimination violate other laws as well. It is possible that an employer who is discriminating on the basis of sexual orientation is also discriminating on the basis of gender.

For example, a male employer asks a lesbian employee to engage in sexual relations with him. She says no, and mentions her sexual orientation. The employer says that he doesn't employ lesbians, and fires her based on her admitted sexual orientation. It could be argued that the employer has also discriminated on the basis of sex, because it's illegal for him to fire the employee because she would not have sexual relations with him. That would be a form of sexual harassment, as previously discussed in this almanac.

Damages

Laws against sexual orientation discrimination are very new, so it is not clear what damages can be received in court. However, it appears that employees can recover their lost wages and other benefits, emotional distress damages, and punitive damages. It unclear whether or not they may recover legal fees and costs.

APPENDIX 1: DIRECTORY OF EEOC OFFICES

EEOC OFFICE	ADDRESS	TELEPHONE	FAX	TTY
Baltimore Field Office	10 S. Howard Street, Third floor Baltimore, MD 21201	800-669-4000	410-962-4270	800-669-6820
Cleveland Field Office	11240 E. 9th Street, Suite 3001 Cleveland, OH 44199	800-669-4000	216-522-7395	800-669-6820
Denver Field Office	303 E. 17th Avenue, Suite 510 Denver, CO 80203	800-669-4000	303-866-1085	800-669-6820
Detroit Field Office	477 Michigan Avenue, Room 865 Detroit, MI 48226	800-669-4000	313-226-4610	800-669-682-
New Orleans Field Office	1555 Poydras Street, Suite 1900 New Orleans, LA 70112	800-669-4000	504-595-2887	800-669-6820
San Antonio Field Office	5410 Fredericksburg Road, Suite 200 San Antonio, TX 78229	800-669-4000	210-281-7690	800-669-6820
Tampa Field Office	501 East Polk Street, Suite 1000 Tampa, FL 33602	800-669-4000	813-228-2841	800-669-6820
Seattle Field Office	909 First Avenue, Suite 400 Seattle, WA 98104	800-669-4000	206-220-6911	800-669-6820

EEOC OFFICE	ADDRESS	TELEPHONE	FAX	TTY
Washington Field Office	1801 L Street NW, Suite 100 Washington, DC 20507	800-669-4000	202-419-0740	800-669-6820
Albuquerque Area Office	505 Marquette NW, Suite 900 Albuquerque, NM 87102	800-669-4000	505-248-5239	800-669-6820
Boston Area Office	475 Government Center Boston, MA 02203	800-669-4000	617-565-3196	800-669-6820
Cincinnati Area Office	550 Main Street, 10th Floor Cincinnati, OH 45202	800-669-4000	513-684-2361	800-669-6820
El Paso Area Office	300 E. Main Drive, Suite 500 El Paso, TX 79901	800-669-4000	915-534-6701	800-669-6820
Jackson Area Office	100 West Capitol Street, Suite 207 Jackson, MS 39269	800-669-4000	601-948-8401	800-669-6820
Kansas City Area Office	4th & State Ave., 9th Floor Kansas City, KS 66101	800-669-4000	913-551-6957	800-669-6820
Little Rock Area Office	820 Louisiana Street, Suite 200 Little Rock, AR 72201	800-669-4000	501-324-5991	800-669-6820
Louisville Area Office	600 Dr. Martin Luther King Jr. Blvd. Suite 268 Louisville, KY 40202	800-669-4000	502-582-5895	800-669-6820
Milwaukee Area Office	310 West Wisconsin Ave., Suite 800 Milwaukee, WI 53203	800-669-4000	414-297-4133	800-669-6820
Minneapolis Area Office	330 South Second Ave., Suite 430 Minneapolis, MN 55401	800-669-4000	612-335-4044	800-669-6820

EEOC OFFICE	ADDRESS	TELEPHONE	FAX	TTY
Nashville Area Office	50 Vantage Way, Suite 202 Nashville, TN 37228	800-669-4000	615-736-2107	800-669-6820
Newark Area Office	One Newark Center, 21st Floor Newark, NJ 07102	800-669-4000	973-645-4524	800-669-6820
Oklahoma Area Office	215 Dean A. McGee Ave., Suite 524 Oklahoma City, OK 73102	800-669-4000	405-231-4140	800-668-6820
Pittsburgh Area Office	1001 Liberty Avenue, Suite 300 Pittsburgh, PA 15222	800-669-4000	412-644-2664	800-669-6820
Raleigh Area Office	1309 Annapolis Drive Raleigh, NC 27608	800-669-4000	919-856-4151	800-669-6820
Buffalo Local office	6 Fountain Plaza, Suite 350 Buffalo, NY 14202	800-669-4000	716-551-4387	800-669-6820
Fresno Local Office	2300 Tulare Street, Suite 215 Fresno, CA 93721	800-669-4000	559-487-5053	800-669-6820
Greensboro Local Office	2303 W. Meadowview Rd., Suite 201 Greensboro, NC 27407	800-669-4000	336-547-4032	800-669-6820
Greenville Local Office	301 N. Main Street, Suite 1402 Greenville, SC 29601	800-669-4000	864-241-4416	800-669-6820
Honolulu Local Office	300 Ala Moana Blvd., Room 7-127 Honolulu, HI 96850	800-669-4000	808-541-3390	800-669-6820
Las Vegas Local Office	333 Las Vegas Blvd. S., Suite 8112 Las Vegas, NV 89101	800-669-4000	702-388-5094	800-669-6820

EEOC OFFICE	ADDRESS	TELEPHONE	FAX	TTY
Mobile Local Office	63 South Royal Street, Suite 504 Mobile, AL 36602	800-669-4000	251-690-2581	800-669-6820
Norfolk Local Office	200 Granby Street, Suite 739 Norfolk, VA 23510	800-669-4000	757-441-6720	800-669-6820
Oakland Local Office	1301 Clay Street, Suite 1170-N Oakland, CA 94612	800-669-4000	510-637-3235	800-669-6820
Richmond Local Office	830 East Main Street, 6th Floor Richmond, VA 23219	800-669-4000	804-771-2222	800-669-6820
San Diego Local Office	401 B. Street, Suite 510 San Diego, CA 92101	800-669-4000	619-557-7274	800-669-6820
San Jose Local Office	96 N. Third Street, Suite 200 San Jose, CA 95112	800-669-4000	408-291-4539	800-669-6820
San Juan Local Office	525 F.D. Roosevelt Ave. Plaza Las Americas, Suite 1202 San Juan, Puerto Rico 00918	800-669-4000	787-771-1485	800-668-6820
Savannah Local Office	410 Mall Boulevard, Suite G Savannah, GA 31406	800-669-4000	912-652-4248	800-669-6820
Atlanta District Office	100 Alabama Street, Suite 4R30 Atlanta, GA 30303	800-669-4000	404-562-6909	800-669-6820
Birmingham District Office	1130 22nd Street South, Suite 2000 Birmingham, AL 35205	800-669-4000	205-212-2105	800-669-6820
Charlotte District Office	129 West Trade Street, Suite 400 Charlotte, NC 28202	800-669-4000	704-344-6734	800-669-6820
Chicago District Office	500 West Madison Street, Suite 2800 Chicago, IL 60661	800-669-4000	312-886-1168	800-669-682-

EEOC OFFICE	ADDRESS	TELEPHONE	FAX	TTY
Dallas District Office	207 S. Houston Street, 3rd Floor Dallas, TX 75202	800-669-4000	214-253-2720	800-669-6820
Houston District Office	1919 Smith Street, 6th Floor Houston, TX 77002	800-669-4000	713-209-3381	800-669-6820
Indianapolis District Office	101 W. Ohio Street, Suite 1900 Indianapolis, IN 46204	800-669-4000	317-226-7953	800-669-6820
Los Angeles District Office	255 E. Temple, 4th Floor Los Angeles, CA 90012	800-669-4000	213-894-1118	800-669-6820
Memphis District Office	1407 Union Avenue, Suite 621 Memphis, TN 38104	800-669-4000	901-544-0111	800-669-6820
Miami District Office	2 South Biscayne Blvd., Suite 2700 Miami, FL 33131	800-669-4000	305-808-1855	800-669-6820
New York District Office	33 Whitehall Street New York, NY 10004	800-669-4000	212-336-3790	800-669-6820
Philadelphia District Office	801 Market Street, Suite 1300 Philadelphia, PA 19107	800-669-4000	215-440-2606	800-669-6820
Phoenix District Office	3300 North Central Ave., Suite 690 Phoenix, AZ 85012	800-669-4000	602-640-5071	800-669-6820
San Francisco District Office	350 The Embarcadero, Suite 500 San Francisco, CA 94105	800-669-4000	415-625-5609	800-669-6820
St. Louis District Office	122 Spruce Street, Room 8.100 St. Louis, MO 63103	800-669-4000	314-539-7894	800-669-6820

Source: U.S. Equal Employment Opportunity Commission.

APPENDIX 2: TITLE VII OF THE CIVIL RIGHTS ACT OF 1964

An Act:

To enforce the constitutional right to vote, to confer jurisdiction upon the district courts of the United States to provide injunctive relief against discrimination in public accommodations, to authorize the attorney General to institute suits to protect constitutional rights in public facilities and public education, to extend the Commission on Civil Rights, to prevent discrimination in federally assisted programs, to establish a Commission on Equal Employment Opportunity, and for other purposes.

Be it enacted by the Senate and House of Representatives of the United States of America in Congress assembled, That this Act may be cited as the "Civil Rights Act of 1964."

DEFINITIONS

SECTION 2000E. [SECTION 701]

For the purposes of this subchapter—

(a) The term "person" includes one or more individuals, governments, governmental agencies, political subdivisions, labor unions, partnerships, associations, corporations, legal representatives, mutual companies, joint-stock companies, trusts, unincorporated organizations, trustees, trustees in cases under title 11 [bankruptcy], or receivers.

(b) The term "employer" means a person engaged in an industry affecting commerce who has fifteen or more employees for each working day in each of twenty or more calendar weeks in the current or preceding calendar year, and any agent of such a person, but such term does not include (1) the United States, a corporation wholly owned by the Government of the United States, an Indian tribe, or any department or agency of the District of Columbia subject by statute to procedures of the competitive service (as defined in section 2102 of title 5 [of the United States Code]), or (2) a bona fide private membership club (other than a labor organization) which is exempt from taxation under section 501(c) of title 26 [the Internal Revenue Code of 1954], except that during the first year after March 24, 1972 [the date of enactment of the Equal Employment Opportunity Act of 1972], persons having fewer than twenty-five employees (and their agents) shall not be considered employers.

(c) The term "employment agency" means any person regularly undertaking with or without compensation to procure employees for an employer or to procure for employees opportunities to work for an employer and includes an agent of such a person.

(d) The term "labor organization" means a labor organization engaged in an industry affecting commerce, and any agent of such an organization, and includes any organization of any kind, any agency, or employee representation committee, group, association, or plan so engaged in which employees participate and which exists for the purpose, in whole or in part, of dealing with employers concerning grievances, labor disputes, wages, rates of pay, hours, or other terms or conditions of employment, and any conference, general committee, joint or system board, or joint council so engaged which is subordinate to a national or international labor organization.

(e) A labor organization shall be deemed to be engaged in an industry affecting commerce if (1) it maintains or operates a hiring hall or hiring office which procures employees for an employer or procures for employees opportunities to work for an employer, or (2) the number of its members (or, where it is a labor organization composed of other labor organizations or their representatives, if the aggregate number of the members of such other labor organization) is (A) twenty-five or more during the first year after March 24, 1972 [the date of enactment of the Equal Employment Opportunity Act of 1972], or (B) fifteen or more thereafter, and such labor organization—

(1) is the certified representative of employees under the provisions of the National Labor Relations Act, as amended [29 U.S.C. § 151 et seq.], or the Railway Labor Act, as amended [45 U.S.C. § 151 et seq.];

(2) although not certified, is a national or international labor organization or a local labor organization recognized or acting as

the representative of employees of an employer or employers engaged in an industry affecting commerce; or

(3) has chartered a local labor organization or subsidiary body which is representing or actively seeking to represent employees of employers within the meaning of paragraph (1) or (2); or

(4) has been chartered by a labor organization representing or actively seeking to represent employees within the meaning of paragraph (1) or (2) as the local or subordinate body through which such employees may enjoy membership or become affiliated with such labor organization; or

(5) is a conference, general committee, joint or system board, or joint council subordinate to a national or international labor organization, which includes a labor organization engaged in an industry affecting commerce within the meaning of any of the preceding paragraphs of this subsection.

(f) The term "employee" means an individual employed by an employer, except that the term "employee" shall not include any person elected to public office in any State or political subdivision of any State by the qualified voters thereof, or any person chosen by such officer to be on such officer's personal staff, or an appointee on the policy making level or an immediate adviser with respect to the exercise of the constitutional or legal powers of the office. The exemption set forth in the preceding sentence shall not include employees subject to the civil service laws of a State government, governmental agency or political subdivision. With respect to employment in a foreign country, such term includes an individual who is a citizen of the United States.

(g) The term "commerce" means trade, traffic, commerce, transportation, transmission, or communication among the several States; or between a State and any place outside thereof; or within the District of Columbia, or a possession of the United States; or between points in the same State but through a point outside thereof.

(h) The term "industry affecting commerce" means any activity, business, or industry in commerce or in which a labor dispute would hinder or obstruct commerce or the free flow of commerce and includes any activity or industry "affecting commerce" within the meaning of the Labor-Management Reporting and Disclosure Act of 1959 [29 U.S.C. § 401 et seq.], and further includes any governmental industry, business, or activity.

(i) The term "State" includes a State of the United States, the District of Columbia, Puerto Rico, the Virgin Islands, American Samoa, Guam,

Wake Island, the Canal Zone, and Outer Continental Shelf lands defined in the Outer Continental Shelf Lands Act [43 U.S.C. § 1331 et seq.].

(j) The term "religion" includes all aspects of religious observance and practice, as well as belief, unless an employer demonstrates that he is unable to reasonably accommodate to an employee's or prospective employee's religious observance or practice without undue hardship on the conduct of the employer's business.

(k) The terms "because of sex" or "on the basis of sex" include, but are not limited to, because of or on the basis of pregnancy, childbirth, or related medical conditions; and women affected by pregnancy, childbirth, or related medical conditions shall be treated the same for all employment-related purposes, including receipt of benefits under fringe benefit programs, as other persons not so affected but similar in their ability or inability to work, and nothing in section 2000e-2(h) of this title [section 703(h)] shall be interpreted to permit otherwise. This subsection shall not require an employer to pay for health insurance benefits for abortion, except where the life of the mother would be endangered if the fetus were carried to term, or except where medical complications have arisen from an abortion: Provided, That nothing herein shall preclude an employer from providing abortion benefits or otherwise affect bargaining agreements in regard to abortion.

(l) The term "complaining party" means the Commission, the Attorney General, or a person who may bring an action or proceeding under this subchapter.

(m) The term "demonstrates" means meets the burdens of production and persuasion.

(n) The term "respondent" means an employer, employment agency, labor organization, joint labor–management committee controlling apprenticeship or other training or retraining program, including an on-the-job training program, or Federal entity subject to section 2000e-16 of this title.

EXEMPTION

SECTION 2000E-1. [SECTION 702]

(a) This subchapter shall not apply to an employer with respect to the employment of aliens outside any State, or to a religious corporation, association, educational institution, or society with respect to the employment of individuals of a particular religion to perform work connected with the carrying on by such corporation, association, educational institution, or society of its activities.

(b) It shall not be unlawful under section 2000e-2 or 2000e-3 of this title [section 703 or 704] for an employer (or a corporation controlled by an employer), labor organization, employment agency, or joint labor-management committee controlling apprenticeship or other training or retraining (including on-the-job training programs) to take any action otherwise prohibited by such section, with respect to an employee in a workplace in a foreign country if compliance with such section would cause such employer (or such corporation), such organization, such agency, or such committee to violate the law of the foreign country in which such workplace is located.

(c) (1) If an employer controls a corporation whose place of incorporation is a foreign country, any practice prohibited by section 2000e-2 or 2000e-3 of this title [section 703 or 704] engaged in by such corporation shall be presumed to be engaged in by such employer.

(c) (2) Sections 2000e-2 and 2000e-3 of this title [sections 703 and 704] shall not apply with respect to the foreign operations of an employer that is a foreign person not controlled by an American employer.

(c) (3) For purposes of this subsection, the determination of whether an employer controls a corporation shall be based on—

(A) the interrelation of operations;

(B) the common management;

(C) the centralized control of labor relations; and

(D) the common ownership or financial control, of the employer and the corporation.

UNLAWFUL EMPLOYMENT PRACTICES

SECTION 2000E-2. [SECTION 703]

(a) It shall be an unlawful employment practice for an employer—

(1) to fail or refuse to hire or to discharge any individual, or otherwise to discriminate against any individual with respect to his compensation, terms, conditions, or privileges of employment, because of such individual's race, color, religion, sex, or national origin; or

(2) to limit, segregate, or classify his employees or applicants for employment in any way which would deprive or tend to deprive any individual of employment opportunities or otherwise adversely affect his status as an employee, because of such individual's race, color, religion, sex, or national origin.

(b) It shall be an unlawful employment practice for an employment agency to fail or refuse to refer for employment, or otherwise to discriminate against, any individual because of his race, color, religion, sex, or national origin, or to classify or refer for employment any individual on the basis of his race, color, religion, sex, or national origin.

(c) It shall be an unlawful employment practice for a labor organization—

(1) to exclude or to expel from its membership, or otherwise to discriminate against, any individual because of his race, color, religion, sex, or national origin;

(2) to limit, segregate, or classify its membership or applicants for membership, or to classify or fail or refuse to refer for employment any individual, in any way which would deprive or tend to deprive any individual of employment opportunities, or would limit such employment opportunities or otherwise adversely affect his status as an employee or as an applicant for employment, because of such individual's race, color, religion, sex, or national origin; or

(3) to cause or attempt to cause an employer to discriminate against an individual in violation of this section.

(d) It shall be an unlawful employment practice for any employer, labor organization, or joint labor-management committee controlling apprenticeship or other training or retraining, including on-the-job training programs to discriminate against any individual because of his race, color, religion, sex, or national origin in admission to, or employment in, any program established to provide apprenticeship or other training.

(e) Notwithstanding any other provision of this subchapter

(1) it shall not be an unlawful employment practice for an employer to hire and employ employees, for an employment agency to classify, or refer for employment any individual, for a labor organization to classify its membership or to classify or refer for employment any individual, or for an employer, labor organization, or joint labor-management committee controlling apprenticeship or other training or retraining programs to admit or employ any individual in any such program, on the basis of his religion, sex, or national origin in those certain instances where religion, sex, or national origin is a bona fide occupational qualification reasonably necessary to the normal operation of that particular business or enterprise, and

(2) it shall not be an unlawful employment practice for a school, college, university, or other educational institution or institution of

learning to hire and employ employees of a particular religion if such school, college, university, or other educational institution or institution of learning is, in whole or in substantial part, owned, supported, controlled, or managed by a particular religion or by a particular religious corporation, association, or society, or if the curriculum of such school, college, university, or other educational institution or institution of learning is directed toward the propagation of a particular religion.

(f) As used in this subchapter, the phrase "unlawful employment practice" shall not be deemed to include any action or measure taken by an employer, labor organization, joint labor-management committee, or employment agency with respect to an individual who is a member of the Communist Party of the United States or of any other organization required to register as a Communist-action or Communist-front organization by final order of the Subversive Activities Control Board pursuant to the Subversive Activities Control Act of 1950 [50 U.S.C. § 781 et seq.].

(g) Notwithstanding any other provision of this subchapter, it shall not be an unlawful employment practice for an employer to fail or refuse to hire and employ any individual for any position, for an employer to discharge any individual from any position, or for an employment agency to fail or refuse to refer any individual for employment in any position, or for a labor organization to fail or refuse to refer any individual for employment in any position, if—

(1) the occupancy of such position, or access to the premises in or upon which any part of the duties of such position is performed or is to be performed, is subject to any requirement imposed in the interest of the national security of the United States under any security program in effect pursuant to or administered under any statute of the United States or any Executive order of the President; and

(2) such individual has not fulfilled or has ceased to fulfill that requirement.

(h) Notwithstanding any other provision of this subchapter, it shall not be an unlawful employment practice for an employer to apply different standards of compensation, or different terms, conditions, or privileges of employment pursuant to a bona fide seniority or merit system, or a system which measures earnings by quantity or quality of production or to employees who work in different locations, provided that such differences are not the result of an intention to discriminate because of race, color, religion, sex, or national origin, nor shall it be an unlawful employment practice for an employer to give and to act upon the results of any professionally developed ability test provided that such test, its administration or action upon the results is not designed, intended or used to discriminate because of race, color, religion, sex or national origin. It shall not be an unlawful employment practice under this subchapter for any employer to differentiate upon the basis of sex in determining the amount of the wages or compensation paid or to be paid to employees of such employer if such differentiation is authorized by the provisions of section 206(d) of title 29 [section 6(d) of the Fair Labor Standards Act of 1938, as amended].

(i) Nothing contained in this subchapter shall apply to any business or enterprise on or near an Indian reservation with respect to any publicly announced employment practice of such business or enterprise under which a preferential treatment is given to any individual because he is an Indian living on or near a reservation.

(j) Nothing contained in this subchapter shall be interpreted to require any employer, employment agency, labor organization, or joint labor-management committee subject to this subchapter to grant preferential treatment to any individual or to any group because of the race, color, religion, sex, or national origin of such individual or group on account of an imbalance which may exist with respect to the total number or percentage of persons of any race, color, religion, sex, or national origin employed by any employer, referred or classified for employment by any employment agency or labor organization, admitted to membership or classified by any labor organization, or admitted to, or employed in, any apprenticeship or other training program, in comparison with the total number or percentage of persons of such race, color, religion, sex, or national origin in any community, State, section, or other area, or in the available work force in any community, State, section, or other area.

(k) (1) (A) An unlawful employment practice based on disparate impact is established under this title only if—

> (i) a complaining party demonstrates that a respondent uses a particular employment practice that causes a disparate impact on the basis of race, color, religion, sex, or national origin and the respondent fails to demonstrate that the challenged practice is job related for the position in question and consistent with business necessity; or
>
> (ii) the complaining party makes the demonstration described in subparagraph (C) with respect to an alternative employment

practice and the respondent refuses to adopt such alternative employment practice.

(B) (i) With respect to demonstrating that a particular employment practice causes a disparate impact as described in subparagraph (A)(i), the complaining party shall demonstrate that each particular challenged employment practice causes a disparate impact, except that if the complaining party can demonstrate to the court that the elements of a respondent's decisionmaking process are not capable of separation for analysis, the decisionmaking process may be analyzed as one employment practice.

(ii) If the respondent demonstrates that a specific employment practice does not cause the disparate impact, the respondent shall not be required to demonstrate that such practice is required by business necessity.

(C) The demonstration referred to by subparagraph (A)(ii) shall be in accordance with the law as it existed on June 4, 1989, with respect to the concept of "alternative employment practice".

(2) A demonstration that an employment practice is required by business necessity may not be used as a defense against a claim of intentional discrimination under this title.

(3) Notwithstanding any other provision of this title, a rule barring the employment of an individual who currently and knowingly uses or possesses a controlled substance, as defined in schedules I and II of section 102(6) of the Controlled Substances Act (21 U.S.C. § 802(6)), other than the use or possession of a drug taken under the supervision of a licensed health care professional, or any other use or possession authorized by the Controlled Substances Act [21 U.S.C. § 801 et seq.] or any other provision of Federal law, shall be considered an unlawful employment practice under this title only if such rule is adopted or applied with an intent to discriminate because of race, color, religion, sex, or national origin.

(l) It shall be an unlawful employment practice for a respondent, in connection with the selection or referral of applicants or candidates for employment or promotion, to adjust the scores of, use different cutoff scores for, or otherwise alter the results of, employment related tests on the basis of race, color, religion, sex, or national origin.

(m) Except as otherwise provided in this title, an unlawful employment practice is established when the complaining party demonstrates that race, color, religion, sex, or national origin was a motivating factor for any employment practice, even though other factors also motivated the practice.

(n) (1) (A) Notwithstanding any other provision of law, and except as provided in paragraph (2), an employment practice that implements and is within the scope of a litigated or consent judgment or order that resolves a claim of employment discrimination under the Constitution or Federal civil rights laws may not be challenged under the circumstances described in subparagraph (B).

(B) A practice described in subparagraph (A) may not be challenged in a claim under the Constitution or Federal civil rights laws—

(i) by a person who, prior to the entry of the judgment or order described in subparagraph (A), had—

(I) actual notice of the proposed judgment or order sufficient to apprise such person that such judgment or order might adversely affect the interests and legal rights of such person and that an opportunity was available to present objections to such judgment or order by a future date certain; and

(II) a reasonable opportunity to present objections to such judgment or order; or

(ii) by a person whose interests were adequately represented by another person who had previously challenged the judgment or order on the same legal grounds and with a similar factual situation, unless there has been an intervening change in law or fact.

(2) Nothing in this subsection shall be construed to—

(A) alter the standards for intervention under rule 24 of the Federal Rules of Civil Procedure or apply to the rights of parties who have successfully intervened pursuant to such rule in the proceeding in which the parties intervened;

(B) apply to the rights of parties to the action in which a litigated or consent judgment or order was entered, or of members of a class represented or sought to be represented in such action, or of members of a group on whose behalf relief was sought in such action by the Federal Government;

(C) prevent challenges to a litigated or consent judgment or order on the ground that such judgment or order was obtained through collusion or fraud, or is transparently invalid or was entered by a court lacking subject matter jurisdiction; or

(D) authorize or permit the denial to any person of the due process of law required by the Constitution.

(3) Any action not precluded under this subsection that challenges an employment consent judgment or order described in paragraph (1) shall be brought in the court, and if possible before the judge, that entered such judgment or order. Nothing in this subsection shall preclude a transfer of such action pursuant to section 1404 of title 28, United States Code.

OTHER UNLAWFUL EMPLOYMENT PRACTICES

SECTION 2000E-3. [SECTION 704]

(a) It shall be an unlawful employment practice for an employer to discriminate against any of his employees or applicants for employment, for an employment agency, or joint labor–management committee controlling apprenticeship or other training or retraining, including on-the-job training programs, to discriminate against any individual, or for a labor organization to discriminate against any member thereof or applicant for membership, because he has opposed any practice made an unlawful employment practice by this subchapter, or because he has made a charge, testified, assisted, or participated in any manner in an investigation, proceeding, or hearing under this subchapter.

(b) It shall be an unlawful employment practice for an employer, labor organization, employment agency, or joint labor-management committee controlling apprenticeship or other training or retraining, including on-the-job training programs, to print or publish or cause to be printed or published any notice or advertisement relating to employment by such an employer or membership in or any classification or referral for employment by such a labor organization, or relating to any classification or referral for employment by such an employment agency, or relating to admission to, or employment in, any program established to provide apprenticeship or other training by such a joint labor-management committee, indicating any preference, limitation, specification, or discrimination, based on race, color, religion, sex, or national origin, except that such a notice or advertisement may indicate a preference, limitation, specification, or discrimination based on religion, sex, or national origin when religion, sex, or national origin is a bona fide occupational qualification for employment.

EQUAL EMPLOYMENT OPPORTUNITY COMMISSION

SECTION 2000E-4. [SECTION 705]

(a) There is hereby created a Commission to be known as the Equal Employment Opportunity Commission, which shall be composed of five members, not more than three of whom shall be members of the same political party. Members of the Commission shall be appointed by the President by and with the advice and consent of the Senate for a term of five years. Any individual chosen to fill a vacancy shall be appointed only for the unexpired term of the member whom he shall succeed, and all members of the Commission shall continue to serve until their successors are appointed and qualified, except that no such member of the Commission shall continue to serve (1) for more than sixty days when the Congress is in session unless a nomination to fill such vacancy shall have been submitted to the Senate, or (2) after the adjournment sine die of the session of the Senate in which such nomination was submitted. The President shall designate one member to serve as Chairman of the Commission, and one member to serve as Vice Chairman. The Chairman shall be responsible on behalf of the Commission for the administrative operations of the Commission, and, except as provided in subsection (b) of this section, shall appoint, in accordance with the provisions of title 5 [United States Code] governing appointments in the competitive service, such officers, agents, attorneys, administrative law judges [hearing examiners], and employees as he deems necessary to assist it in the performance of its functions and to fix their compensation in accordance with the provisions of chapter 51 and subchapter III of chapter 53 of title 5 [United States Code], relating to classification and General Schedule pay rates: Provided, That assignment, removal, and compensation of administrative law judges [hearing examiners] shall be in accordance with sections 3105, 3344, 5372, and 7521 of title 5 [United States Code].

(b) (1) There shall be a General Counsel of the Commission appointed by the President, by and with the advice and consent of the Senate, for a term of four years. The General Counsel shall have responsibility for the conduct of litigation as provided in sections 2000e-5 and 2000e-6 of this title [sections 706 and 707]. The General Counsel shall have such other duties as the Commission may prescribe or as may be provided by law and shall concur with the Chairman of the Commission on the appointment and supervision of regional attorneys. The General Counsel of the Commission on the effective date of this Act shall continue in such position and perform the functions specified in this subsection until a successor is appointed and qualified.

(2) Attorneys appointed under this section may, at the direction of the Commission, appear for and represent the Commission in any case in court, provided that the Attorney General shall conduct all litigation to which the Commission is a party in the Supreme Court pursuant to this subchapter.

(c) A vacancy in the Commission shall not impair the right of the remaining members to exercise all the powers of the Commission and three members thereof shall constitute a quorum.

(d) The Commission shall have an official seal which shall be judicially noticed.

(e) The Commission shall at the close of each fiscal year report to the Congress and to the President concerning the action it has taken [the names, salaries, and duties of all individuals in its employ] and the moneys it has disbursed. It shall make such further reports on the cause of and means of eliminating discrimination and such recommendations for further legislation as may appear desirable.

(f) The principal office of the Commission shall be in or near the District of Columbia, but it may meet or exercise any or all its powers at any other place. The Commission may establish such regional or State offices as it deems necessary to accomplish the purpose of this subchapter.

(g) The Commission shall have power—

(1) to cooperate with and, with their consent, utilize regional, State, local, and other agencies, both public and private, and individuals;

(2) to pay to witnesses whose depositions are taken or who are summoned before the Commission or any of its agents the same witness and mileage fees as are paid to witnesses in the courts of the United States;

(3) to furnish to persons subject to this subchapter such technical assistance as they may request to further their compliance with this subchapter or an order issued thereunder;

(4) upon the request of (i) any employer, whose employees or some of them, or (ii) any labor organization, whose members or some of them, refuse or threaten to refuse to cooperate in effectuating the provisions of this subchapter, to assist in such effectuation by conciliation or such other remedial action as is provided by this subchapter;

(5) to make such technical studies as are appropriate to effectuate the purposes and policies of this subchapter and to make the results of such studies available to the public;

(6) to intervene in a civil action brought under section 2000e-5 of this title [section 706] by an aggrieved party against a respondent other than a government, governmental agency or political subdivision.

(h) (1) The Commission shall, in any of its educational or promotional activities, cooperate with other departments and agencies in the performance of such educational and promotional activities.

(2) In exercising its powers under this title, the Commission shall carry out educational and outreach activities (including dissemination of information in languages other than English) targeted to—

(A) individuals who historically have been victims of employment discrimination and have not been equitably served by the Commission; and

(B) individuals on whose behalf the Commission has authority to enforce any other law prohibiting employment discrimination, concerning rights and obligations under this title or such law, as the case may be.

(i) All officers, agents, attorneys, and employees of the Commission shall be subject to the provisions of section 7324 of title 5 [section 9 of the Act of August 2, 1939, as amended (the Hatch Act)], notwithstanding any exemption contained in such section.

(j) (1) The Commission shall establish a Technical Assistance Training Institute, through which the Commission shall provide technical assistance and training regarding the laws and regulations enforced by the Commission.

(2) An employer or other entity covered under this title shall not be excused from compliance with the requirements of this title because of any failure to receive technical assistance under this subsection.

(3) There are authorized to be appropriated to carry out this subsection such sums as may be necessary for fiscal year 1992.

ENFORCEMENT PROVISIONS

SECTION 2000E-5. [SECTION 706]

(a) The Commission is empowered, as hereinafter provided, to prevent any person from engaging in any unlawful employment practice as set forth in section 2000e-2 or 2000e-3 of this title [section 703 or 704].

(b) Whenever a charge is filed by or on behalf of a person claiming to be aggrieved, or by a member of the Commission, alleging that an employer, employment agency, labor organization, or joint labor-management committee controlling apprenticeship or other training or retraining, including on- the-job training programs, has engaged in an unlawful employment practice, the Commission shall serve a notice of the charge (including the date, place and circumstances of the alleged unlawful employment practice) on such employer, employment agency, labor organization, or joint labor-management committee (hereinafter referred to as the "respondent") within ten days, and shall make an investigation thereof. Charges shall be in writing under oath or affirmation and shall contain such information and be in such form as the Commission requires. Charges shall not be made public by the Commission. If the Commission determines after such investigation that there is not reasonable cause to believe that the charge is true, it shall dismiss the charge and promptly notify the person claiming to be aggrieved and the respondent of its action. In determining whether reasonable cause exists, the Commission shall accord substantial weight to final findings and orders made by State or local authorities in proceedings commenced under State or local law pursuant to the requirements of subsections (c) and (d) of this section. If the Commission determines after such investigation that there is reasonable cause to believe that the charge is true, the Commission shall endeavor to eliminate any such alleged unlawful employment practice by informal methods of conference, conciliation, and persuasion. Nothing said or done during and as a part of such informal endeavors may be made public by the Commission, its officers or employees, or used as evidence in a subsequent proceeding without the written consent of the persons concerned. Any person who makes public information in violation of this subsection shall be fined not more than $1, 000 or imprisoned for not more than one year, or both. The Commission shall make its determination as practicable, not later than one hundred and twenty days from the filing of the charge or, where applicable under subsection (c) or (d) of this section, from the date upon which the Commission is authorized to take action with respect to the charge.

(c) In the case of an alleged unlawful employment practice occurring in a State, or political subdivision of a State, which has a State or local law prohibiting the unlawful employment practice alleged and establishing or authorizing a State or local authority to grant or seek relief from such practice or to institute criminal proceedings with respect thereto upon receiving notice thereof, no charge may be filed under subsection (a) of this section by the person aggrieved before the expiration of sixty days after proceedings have been commenced under the State or local law, unless such proceedings have been earlier terminated, provided that such sixty-day period shall be extended to one hundred and twenty days during the first year after the effective date of such State or local law. If any requirement for the commencement of such proceedings is imposed by a State or local authority other than a requirement of the filing of a written and signed statement of the facts upon which the proceeding is based, the proceeding shall be deemed to have been commenced for the purposes of this subsection at the time such statement is sent by registered mail to the appropriate State or local authority.

(d) In the case of any charge filed by a member of the Commission alleging an unlawful employment practice occurring in a State or political subdivision of a State which has a State or local law prohibiting the practice alleged and establishing or authorizing a State or local authority to grant or seek relief from such practice or to institute criminal proceedings with respect thereto upon receiving notice thereof, the Commission shall, before taking any action with respect to such charge, notify the appropriate State or local officials and, upon request, afford them a reasonable time, but not less than sixty days (provided that such sixty-day period shall be extended to one hundred and twenty days during the first year after the effective day of such State or local law), unless a shorter period is requested, to act under such State or local law to remedy the practice alleged.

(e) (1) A charge under this section shall be filed within one hundred and eighty days after the alleged unlawful employment practice occurred and notice of the charge (including the date, place and circumstances of the alleged unlawful employment practice) shall be served upon the person against whom such charge is made within ten days thereafter, except that in a case of an unlawful employment practice with respect to which the person aggrieved has initially instituted proceedings with a State or local agency with authority to grant or seek relief from such practice or to institute criminal proceedings with respect thereto upon receiving notice thereof, such charge shall be filed by or on behalf of the person aggrieved within three hundred days after the alleged unlawful employment practice occurred, or within thirty days after receiving notice that the State or local agency has terminated the proceedings under the State or local law, whichever is earlier, and a copy of such charge shall be filed by the Commission with the State or local agency.

(2) For purposes of this section, an unlawful employment practice occurs, with respect to a seniority system that has been adopted for

an intentionally discriminatory purpose in violation of this title (whether or not that discriminatory purpose is apparent on the face of the seniority provision), when the seniority system is adopted, when an individual becomes subject to the seniority system, or when a person aggrieved is injured by the application of the seniority system or provision of the system.

(f) (1) If within thirty days after a charge is filed with the Commission or within thirty days after expiration of any period of reference under subsection (c) or (d) of this section, the Commission has been unable to secure from the respondent a conciliation agreement acceptable to the Commission, the Commission may bring a civil action against any respondent not a government, governmental agency, or political subdivision named in the charge. In the case of a respondent which is a government, governmental agency, or political subdivision, if the Commission has been unable to secure from the respondent a conciliation agreement acceptable to the Commission, the Commission shall take no further action and shall refer the case to the Attorney General who may bring a civil action against such respondent in the appropriate United States district court. The person or persons aggrieved shall have the right to intervene in a civil action brought by the Commission or the Attorney General in a case involving a government, governmental agency, or political subdivision. If a charge filed with the Commission pursuant to subsection (b) of this section, is dismissed by the Commission, or if within one hundred and eighty days from the filing of such charge or the expiration of any period of reference under subsection (c) or (d) of this section, whichever is later, the Commission has not filed a civil action under this section or the Attorney General has not filed a civil action in a case involving a government, governmental agency, or political subdivision, or the Commission has not entered into a conciliation agreement to which the person aggrieved is a party, the Commission, or the Attorney General in a case involving a government, governmental agency, or political subdivision, shall so notify the person aggrieved and within ninety days after the giving of such notice a civil action may be brought against the respondent named in the charge (A) by the person claiming to be aggrieved or (B) if such charge was filed by a member of the Commission, by any person whom the charge alleges was aggrieved by the alleged unlawful employment practice. Upon application by the complainant and in such circumstances as the court may deem just, the court may appoint an attorney for such complainant and may authorize the commencement of the action without the payment of fees, costs, or security. Upon timely application, the court may, in its discretion, permit the Commission, or the Attorney

General in a case involving a government, governmental agency, or political subdivision, to intervene in such civil action upon certification that the case is of general public importance. Upon request, the court may, in its discretion, stay further proceedings for not more than sixty days pending the termination of State or local proceedings described in subsection (c) or (d) of this section or further efforts of the Commission to obtain voluntary compliance.

(2) Whenever a charge is filed with the Commission and the Commission concludes on the basis of a preliminary investigation that prompt judicial action is necessary to carry out the purposes of this Act, the Commission, or the Attorney General in a case involving a government, governmental agency, or political subdivision, may bring an action for appropriate temporary or preliminary relief pending final disposition of such charge. Any temporary restraining order or other order granting preliminary or temporary relief shall be issued in accordance with rule 65 of the Federal Rules of Civil Procedure. It shall be the duty of a court having jurisdiction over proceedings under this section to assign cases for hearing at the earliest practicable date and to cause such cases to be in every way expedited.

(3) Each United States district court and each United States court of a place subject to the jurisdiction of the United States shall have jurisdiction of actions brought under this subchapter. Such an action may be brought in any judicial district in the State in which the unlawful employment practice is alleged to have been committed, in the judicial district in which the employment records relevant to such practice are maintained and administered, or in the judicial district in which the aggrieved person would have worked but for the alleged unlawful employment practice, but if the respondent is not found within any such district, such an action may be brought within the judicial district in which the respondent has his principal office. For purposes of sections 1404 and 1406 of title 28 [of the United States Code], the judicial district in which the respondent has his principal office shall in all cases be considered a district in which the action might have been brought.

(4) It shall be the duty of the chief judge of the district (or in his absence, the acting chief judge) in which the case is pending immediately to designate a judge in such district to hear and determine the case. In the event that no judge in the district is available to hear and determine the case, the chief judge of the district, or the acting chief judge, as the case may be, shall certify this fact to the chief judge of the circuit (or in his absence, the acting chief judge) who shall then designate a district or circuit judge of the circuit to hear and determine the case.

(5) It shall be the duty of the judge designated pursuant to this subsection to assign the case for hearing at the earliest practicable date and to cause the case to be in every way expedited. If such judge has not scheduled the case for trial within one hundred and twenty days after issue has been joined, that judge may appoint a master pursuant to rule 53 of the Federal Rules of Civil Procedure.

(g) (1) If the court finds that the respondent has intentionally engaged in or is intentionally engaging in an unlawful employment practice charged in the complaint, the court may enjoin the respondent from engaging in such unlawful employment practice, and order such affirmative action as may be appropriate, which may include, but is not limited to, reinstatement or hiring of employees, with or without back pay (payable by the employer, employment agency, or labor organization, as the case may be, responsible for the unlawful employment practice), or any other equitable relief as the court deems appropriate. Back pay liability shall not accrue from a date more than two years prior to the filing of a charge with the Commission. Interim earnings or amounts earnable with reasonable diligence by the person or persons discriminated against shall operate to reduce the back pay otherwise allowable.

(2) (A) No order of the court shall require the admission or reinstatement of an individual as a member of a union, or the hiring, reinstatement, or promotion of an individual as an employee, or the payment to him of any back pay, if such individual was refused admission, suspended, or expelled, or was refused employment or advancement or was suspended or discharged for any reason other than discrimination on account of race, color, religion, sex, or national origin or in violation of section 2000e-3(a) of this title [section 704(a)].

(B) On a claim in which an individual proves a violation under section 2000e-2(m) of this title [section 703(m)] and a respondent demonstrates that the respondent would have taken the same action in the absence of the impermissible motivating factor, the court-

(i) may grant declaratory relief, injunctive relief (except as provided in clause (ii)), and attorney's fees and costs demonstrated to be directly attributable only to the pursuit of a claim under section 2000e-2(m) of this title [section 703(m)]; and

(ii) shall not award damages or issue an order requiring any admission, reinstatement, hiring, promotion, or payment, described in subparagraph (A).

(h) The provisions of chapter 6 of title 29 [the Act entitled "An Act to amend the Judicial Code and to define and limit the jurisdiction of courts sitting in equity, and for other purposes, " approved March 23, 1932 (29 U.S.C. § 105-115)] shall not apply with respect to civil actions brought under this section.

(i) In any case in which an employer, employment agency, or labor organization fails to comply with an order of a court issued in a civil action brought under this section, the Commission may commence proceedings to compel compliance with such order.

(j) Any civil action brought under this section and any proceedings brought under subsection (i) of this section shall be subject to appeal as provided in sections 1291 and 1292, title 28 [United States Code].

(k) In any action or proceeding under this subchapter the court, in its discretion, may allow the prevailing party, other than the Commission or the United States, a reasonable attorney's fee (including expert fees) as part of the costs, and the Commission and the United States shall be liable for costs the same as a private person.

CIVIL ACTIONS BY THE ATTORNEY GENERAL

SECTION 2000E-6. [SECTION 707]

(a) Whenever the Attorney General has reasonable cause to believe that any person or group of persons is engaged in a pattern or practice of resistance to the full enjoyment of any of the rights secured by this subchapter, and that the pattern or practice is of such a nature and is intended to deny the full exercise of the rights herein described, the Attorney General may bring a civil action in the appropriate district court of the United States by filing with it a complaint (1) signed by him (or in his absence the Acting Attorney General), (2) setting forth facts pertaining to such pattern or practice, and (3) requesting such relief, including an application for a permanent or temporary injunction, restraining order or other order against the person or persons responsible for such pattern or practice, as he deems necessary to insure the full enjoyment of the rights herein described.

(b) The district courts of the United States shall have and shall exercise jurisdiction of proceedings instituted pursuant to this section, and in any such proceeding the Attorney General may file with the clerk of such court a request that a court of three judges be convened to hear and determine the case. Such request by the Attorney General shall be accompanied by a certificate that, in his opinion, the case is of general public importance. A copy of the certificate and request for a three-judge court shall be immediately furnished by such clerk to the chief judge of the circuit (or in his absence, the presiding circuit judge of the circuit) in which the case is pending. Upon receipt of such request it shall be the duty of the chief judge of the circuit or the presiding circuit judge, as the case may be, to designate immediately three judges in such circuit, of whom at least one shall be a circuit judge and another of whom shall be a district judge of the court in which the proceeding was instituted, to hear and determine such case, and it shall be the duty of the judges so designated to assign the case for hearing at the earliest practicable date, to participate in the hearing and determination thereof, and to cause the case to be in every way expedited. An appeal from the final judgment of such court will lie to the Supreme Court. In the event the Attorney General fails to file such a request in any such proceeding, it shall be the duty of the chief judge of the district (or in his absence, the acting chief judge) in which the case is pending immediately to designate a judge in such district to hear and determine the case. In the event that no judge in the district is available to hear and determine the case, the chief judge of the district, or the acting chief judge, as the case may be, shall certify this fact to the chief judge of the circuit (or in his absence, the acting chief judge) who shall then designate a district or circuit judge of the circuit to hear and determine the case. It shall be the duty of the judge designated pursuant to this section to assign the case for hearing at the earliest practicable date and to cause the case to be in every way expedited.

(c) Effective two years after March 24, 1972 [the date of enactment of the Equal Employment Opportunity Act of 1972], the functions of the Attorney General under this section shall be transferred to the Commission, together with such personnel, property, records, and unexpended balances of appropriations, allocations, and other funds employed, used, held, available, or to be made available in connection with such functions unless the President submits, and neither House of Congress vetoes, a reorganization plan pursuant to chapter 9 of title 5 [United States Code], inconsistent with the provisions of this subsection. The Commission shall carry out such functions in accordance with subsections (d) and (e) of this section.

(d) Upon the transfer of functions provided for in subsection (c) of this section, in all suits commenced pursuant to this section prior to the date of such transfer, proceedings shall continue without abatement, all court orders and decrees shall remain in effect, and the Commission shall be substituted as a party for the United States of America, the Attorney General, or the Acting Attorney General, as appropriate.

(e) Subsequent to March 24, 1972 [the date of enactment of the Equal Employment Opportunity Act of 1972], the Commission shall have authority to investigate and act on a charge of a pattern or practice of discrimination, whether filed by or on behalf of a person claiming to be aggrieved or by a member of the Commission. All such actions shall be conducted in accordance with the procedures set forth in section 2000e-5 of this title [section 706].

EFFECT ON STATE LAWS

SECTION 2000E-7. [SECTION 708]

Nothing in this subchapter shall be deemed to exempt or relieve any person from any liability, duty, penalty, or punishment provided by any present or future law of any State or political subdivision of a State, other than any such law which purports to require or permit the doing of any act which would be an unlawful employment practice under this subchapter.

INVESTIGATIONS, INSPECTIONS, RECORDS, STATE AGENCIES

SECTION 2000E-8. [SECTION 709]

(a) In connection with any investigation of a charge filed under section 2000e-5 of this title [section 706], the Commission or its designated representative shall at all reasonable times have access to, for the purposes of examination, and the right to copy any evidence of any person being investigated or proceeded against that relates to unlawful employment practices covered by this subchapter and is relevant to the charge under investigation.

(b) The Commission may cooperate with State and local agencies charged with the administration of State fair employment practices laws and, with the consent of such agencies, may, for the purpose of carrying out its functions and duties under this subchapter and within the limitation of funds appropriated specifically for such purpose, engage in and contribute to the cost of research and other projects of mutual interest undertaken by such agencies, and utilize the services of such agencies and their employees, and, notwithstanding any other provision of law, pay by advance or reimbursement such agencies and their employees for services rendered to assist the Commission in carrying out this subchapter. In furtherance of such cooperative efforts, the Commission may enter into written agreements with such State or local agencies and such agreements may include provisions under which the Commission shall refrain from processing a charge in any cases or class of cases specified in such agreements or under which the Commission shall relieve any person or class of persons in such State or locality from requirements imposed under this section. The Commission shall rescind any such agreement whenever it determines that the agreement no longer serves the interest of effective enforcement of this subchapter.

(c) Every employer, employment agency, and labor organization subject to this subchapter shall (1) make and keep such records relevant to the determinations of whether unlawful employment practices have been or are being committed, (2) preserve such records for such periods, and (3) make such reports therefrom as the Commission shall prescribe by regulation or order, after public hearing, as reasonable, necessary, or appropriate for the enforcement of this subchapter or the regulations or orders thereunder. The Commission shall, by regulation, require each employer, labor organization, and joint labor-management committee subject to this subchapter which controls an apprenticeship or other training program to maintain such records as are reasonably necessary to carry out the purposes of this subchapter, including, but not limited to, a list of applicants who wish to participate in such program, including the chronological order in which applications were received, and to furnish to the Commission upon request, a detailed description of the manner in which persons are selected to participate in the apprenticeship or other training program. Any employer, employment agency, labor organization, or joint labor-management committee which believes that the application to it of any regulation or order issued under this section would result in undue hardship may apply to the Commission for an exemption from the application of such regulation or order, and, if such application for an exemption is denied, bring a civil action in the United States district court for the district where such records are kept. If the Commission or the court, as the case may be, finds that the application of the regulation or order to the employer, employment agency, or labor organization in question would impose an undue hardship, the Commission or the court, as the case may be, may grant appropriate relief. If any person required to comply with the provisions of this subsection fails or refuses to do so, the United States district court for the district in which such person is found, resides, or transacts business, shall, upon application of the Commission, or the Attorney General in a case involving a government, governmental agency or political subdivision, have jurisdiction to issue to such person an order requiring him to comply.

(d) In prescribing requirements pursuant to subsection (c) of this section, the Commission shall consult with other interested State and

Federal agencies and shall endeavor to coordinate its requirements with those adopted by such agencies. The Commission shall furnish upon request and without cost to any State or local agency charged with the administration of a fair employment practice law information obtained pursuant to subsection (c) of this section from any employer, employment agency, labor organization, or joint labor-management committee subject to the jurisdiction of such agency. Such information shall be furnished on condition that it not be made public by the recipient agency prior to the institution of a proceeding under State or local law involving such information. If this condition is violated by a recipient agency, the Commission may decline to honor subsequent requests pursuant to this subsection.

(e) It shall be unlawful for any officer or employee of the Commission to make public in any manner whatever any information obtained by the Commission pursuant to its authority under this section prior to the institution of any proceeding under this subchapter involving such information. Any officer or employee of the Commission who shall make public in any manner whatever any information in violation of this subsection shall be guilty, of a misdemeanor and upon conviction thereof, shall be fined not more than $1, 000, or imprisoned not more than one year.

INVESTIGATORY POWERS

SECTION 2000E-9. [SECTION 710]

For the purpose of all hearings and investigations conducted by the Commission or its duly authorized agents or agencies, section 161 of title 29 [section 11 of the National Labor Relations Act] shall apply.

POSTING OF NOTICES; PENALTIES

SECTION 2000E-10. [SECTION 711]

(a) Every employer, employment agency, and labor organization, as the case may be, shall post and keep posted in conspicuous places upon its premises where notices to employees, applicants for employment, and members are customarily posted a notice to be prepared or approved by the Commission setting forth excerpts, from or, summaries of, the pertinent provisions of this subchapter and information pertinent to the filing of a complaint.

(b) A willful violation of this section shall be punishable by a fine of not more than $100 for each separate offense.

VETERANS' SPECIAL RIGHTS OR PREFERENCE

SECTION 2000E-11. [SECTION 712]

Nothing contained in this subchapter shall be construed to repeal or modify any Federal, State, territorial, or local law creating special rights or preference for veterans.

RULES AND REGULATIONS

SECTION 2000E-12. [SECTION 713]

(a) The Commission shall have authority from time to time to issue, amend, or rescind suitable procedural regulations to carry out the provisions of this subchapter. Regulations issued under this section shall be in conformity with the standards and limitations of subchapter II of chapter 5 of title 5 [the Administrative Procedure Act].

(b) In any action or proceeding based on any alleged unlawful employment practice, no person shall be subject to any liability or punishment for or on account of (1) the commission by such person of an unlawful employment practice if he pleads and proves that the act or omission complained of was in good faith, in conformity with, and in reliance on any written interpretation or opinion of the Commission, or (2) the failure of such person to publish and file any information required by any provision of this subchapter if he pleads and proves that he failed to publish and file such information in good faith, in conformity with the instructions of the Commission issued under this subchapter regarding the filing of such information. Such a defense, if established, shall be a bar to the action or proceeding, notwithstanding that (A) after such act or omission, such interpretation or opinion is modified or rescinded or is determined by judicial authority to be invalid or of no legal effect, or (B) after publishing or filing the description and annual reports, such publication or filing is determined by judicial authority not to be in conformity with the requirements of this subchapter.

FORCIBLY RESISTING THE COMMISSION OR ITS REPRESENTATIVES

SECTION 2000E-13. [SECTION 714]

The provisions of sections 111 and 1114, title 18 [United States Code], shall apply to officers, agents, and employees of the Commission in the performance of their official duties. Notwithstanding the provisions of sections 111 and 1114 of title 18 [United States Code], whoever in violation of the provisions of section 1114 of such title kills a person while engaged in or on account of the performance of his official functions under this Act shall be punished by imprisonment for any term of years or for life.

TRANSFER OF AUTHORITY

[Administration of the duties of the Equal Employment Opportunity Coordinating Council was transferred to the Equal Employment Opportunity Commission effective July 1, 1978, under the President's Reorganization Plan of 1978.]

EQUAL EMPLOYMENT OPPORTUNITY COORDINATING COUNCIL

SECTION 2000E-14. [SECTION 715]

[There shall be established an Equal Employment Opportunity Coordinating Council (hereinafter referred to in this section as the Council) composed of the Secretary of Labor, the Chairman of the Equal Employment Opportunity Commission, the Attorney General, the Chairman of the United States Civil Service Commission, and the Chairman of the United States Civil Rights Commission, or their respective delegates.]

The Equal Employment Opportunity Commission [Council] shall have the responsibility for developing and implementing agreements, policies and practices designed to maximize effort, promote efficiency, and eliminate conflict, competition, duplication and inconsistency among the operations, functions and jurisdictions of the various departments, agencies and branches of the Federal Government responsible for the implementation and enforcement of equal employment opportunity legislation, orders, and policies. On or before October 1 [July 1] of each year, the Equal Employment Opportunity Commission [Council] shall transmit to the President and to the Congress a report of its activities, together with such recommendations for legislative or administrative changes as it concludes are desirable to further promote the purposes of this section.

EFFECTIVE DATE

SECTION 2000E-15. [SECTION 716]

(a) This title shall become effective one year after the date of its enactment.

(b) Notwithstanding subsection (a), sections of this title other than sections 703, 704, 706, and 707 shall become effective immediately.

(c) The President shall, as soon as feasible after July 2, 1964 [the enactment of this title], convene one or more conferences for the purpose of enabling the leaders of groups whose members will be affected by this subchapter to become familiar with the rights afforded and obligations imposed by its provisions, and for the purpose of making plans which will result in the fair and effective administration of this subchapter when all of its provisions become effective. The President shall invite the participation in such conference or conferences of (1) the members of the President's Committee on Equal Employment Opportunity, (2) the members of the Commission on Civil Rights, (3) representatives of State and local agencies engaged in furthering equal employment opportunity, (4) representatives of private agencies engaged in furthering equal employment opportunity, and (5) representatives of employers, labor organizations, and employment agencies who will be subject to this subchapter.

TRANSFER OF AUTHORITY

[Enforcement of Section 717 was transferred to the Equal Employment Opportunity Commission from the Civil Service Commission (Office of Personnel Management) effective January 1, 1979 under the President's Reorganization Plan No. 1 of 1978.]

EMPLOYMENT BY FEDERAL GOVERNMENT

SECTION 2000E-16. [SECTION 717]

(a) All personnel actions affecting employees or applicants for employment (except with regard to aliens employed outside the limits of the United States) in military departments as defined in section 102 of title 5 [United States Code], in executive agencies [other than the General Accounting Office] as defined in section 105 of title 5 [United States Code] (including employees and applicants for employment who are paid from nonappropriated funds), in the United States Postal Service and the Postal Rate Commission, in those units of the Government of the District of Columbia having positions in the competitive service, and in those units of the legislative and judicial branches of the Federal Government having positions in the competitive service, and in the Library of Congress shall be made free from any discrimination based on race, color, religion, sex, or national origin.

(b) Except as otherwise provided in this subsection, the Equal Employment Opportunity Commission [Civil Service Commission] shall have authority to enforce the provisions of subsection (a) of this section through appropriate remedies, including reinstatement or hiring of employees with or without back pay, as will effectuate the policies of this section, and shall issue such rules, regulations, orders and instructions as it deems necessary and appropriate to carry out its responsibilities under this section. The Equal Employment Opportunity Commission [Civil Service Commission] shall—

(1) be responsible for the annual review and approval of a national and regional equal employment opportunity plan which each department and agency and each appropriate unit referred to in subsection (a) of this section shall submit in order to maintain an affirmative program of equal employment opportunity for all such employees and applicants for employment;

(2) be responsible for the review and evaluation of the operation of all agency equal employment opportunity programs, periodically obtaining and publishing (on at least a semiannual basis) progress reports from each such department, agency, or unit; and

(3) consult with and solicit the recommendations of interested individuals, groups, and organizations relating to equal employment opportunity.

The head of each such department, agency, or unit shall comply with such rules, regulations, orders, and instructions which shall include a provision that an employee or applicant for employment shall be notified of any final action taken on any complaint of discrimination filed by him thereunder. The plan submitted by each department, agency, and unit shall include, but not be limited to—

(1) provision for the establishment of training and education programs designed to provide a maximum opportunity for employees to advance so as to perform at their highest potential; and

(2) a description of the qualifications in terms of training and experience relating to equal employment opportunity for the principal and operating officials of each such department, agency, or unit responsible for carrying out the equal employment opportunity program and of the allocation of personnel and resources proposed by such department, agency, or unit to carry out its equal employment opportunity program. With respect to employment in the Library of Congress, authorities granted in this subsection to the Equal Employment Opportunity Commission [Civil Service Commission] shall be exercised by the Librarian of Congress.

(c) Within 90 days of receipt of notice of final action taken by a department, agency, or unit referred to in subsection (a) of this section, or by the Equal Employment Opportunity Commission [Civil Service Commission] upon an appeal from a decision or order of such department, agency, or unit on a complaint of discrimination based on race, color, religion, sex or national origin, brought pursuant to subsection (a) of this section,

Executive Order 11478 or any succeeding Executive orders, or after one hundred and eighty days from the filing of the initial charge with the department, agency, or unit or with the Equal Employment Opportunity Commission [Civil Service Commission] on appeal from a decision or order of such department, agency, or unit until such time as final action may be taken by a department, agency, or unit, an employee or applicant for employment, if aggrieved by the final disposition of his complaint, or by the failure to take final action on his complaint, may file a civil action as provided in section 2000e-5 of this title [section 706], in which civil action the head of the department, agency, or unit, as appropriate, shall be the defendant.

(d) The provisions of section 2000e-5(f) through (k) of this title [section 706(f) through (k)], as applicable, shall govern civil actions brought hereunder, and the same interest to compensate for delay in payment shall be available as in cases involving nonpublic parties.

(e) Nothing contained in this Act shall relieve any Government agency or official of its or his primary responsibility to assure nondiscrimination in employment as required by the Constitution and statutes or of its or his responsibilities under Executive Order 11478 relating to equal employment opportunity in the Federal Government.

SPECIAL PROVISIONS WITH RESPECT TO DENIAL, TERMINATION, AND SUSPENSION OF GOVERNMENT CONTRACTS

SECTION 2000E-17. [SECTION 718]

No Government contract, or portion thereof, with any employer, shall be denied, withheld, terminated, or suspended, by any agency or officer of the United States under any equal employment opportunity law or order, where such employer has an affirmative action plan which has previously been accepted by the Government for the same facility within the past twelve months without first according such employer full hearing and adjudication under the provisions of section 554 of title 5 [United States Code], and the following pertinent sections: Provided, That if such employer has deviated substantially from such previously agreed to affirmative action plan, this section shall not apply: Provided further, That for the purposes of this section an affirmative action plan shall be deemed to have been accepted by the Government at the time the appropriate compliance agency has accepted such plan unless within forty-five days thereafter the Office of Federal Contract Compliance has disapproved such plan.

APPENDIX 3: SELECTED PROVISIONS - THE CIVIL RIGHTS ACT OF 1991

An Act:

To amend the Civil Rights Act of 1964 to strengthen and improve Federal civil rights laws, to provide for damages in cases of intentional employment discrimination, to clarify provisions regarding disparate impact actions, and for other purposes.

Be it enacted by the Senate and House of Representatives of the United States of America in Congress assembled, This Act may be cited as the "Civil Rights Act of 1991."

FINDINGS

SECTION 2. [42 U.S.C. § 1981 NOTE]

The Congress finds that—-

(1) additional remedies under Federal law are needed to deter unlawful harassment and intentional discrimination in the workplace;

(2) the decision of the Supreme Court in *Wards Cove Packing Co. v. Atonio*, 490 U.S. 642 (1989) has weakened the scope and effectiveness of Federal civil rights protections; and

(3) legislation is necessary to provide additional protections against unlawful discrimination in employment.

PURPOSES

SECTION 3 [42 U.S.C. § 1981 NOTE]

The purposes of this Act are—

(1) to provide appropriate remedies for intentional discrimination and unlawful harassment in the workplace;

(2) to codify the concepts of "business necessity" and "job related" enunciated by the Supreme Court in *Griggs v. Duke Power Co.*, 401 U.S. 424 (1971), and in the other Supreme Court decisions prior to *Wards Cove Packing Co. v. Atonio*, 490 U.S. 642 (1989);

(3) to confirm statutory authority and provide statutory guidelines for the adjudication of disparate impact suits under title VII of the Civil Rights Act of 1964 (42 U.S.C. § 2000e et seq.); and

(4) to respond to recent decisions of the Supreme Court by expanding the scope of relevant civil rights statutes in order to provide adequate protection to victims of discrimination.

TITLE I—FEDERAL CIVIL RIGHTS REMEDIES

SECTION 102. DAMAGES IN CASES OF INTENTIONAL DISCRIMINATION

The Revised Statutes are amended by inserting after section 1977 (42 U.S.C. § 1981) the following new section:

"SEC. 1977A. DAMAGES IN CASES OF INTENTIONAL DISCRIMINATION IN EMPLOYMENT. [42 U.S.C. § 1981a]

"(a) Right of Recovery.—

"(1) Civil Rights.— In an action brought by a complaining party under section 706 or 717 of the Civil Rights Act of 1964 (42 U.S.C. § 2000e-5) against a respondent who engaged in unlawful intentional discrimination (not an employment practice that is unlawful because of its disparate impact) prohibited under section 703, 704, or 717 of the Act (42 U.S.C. § 2000e-2 or 2000e-3), and provided that the complaining party cannot recover under section 1977 of the Revised Statutes (42 U.S.C. § 1981), the complaining party may recover compensatory and punitive damages as allowed in subsection (b), in addition to any relief authorized by section 706(g) of the Civil Rights Act of 1964, from the respondent.

"(b) Compensatory and Punitive Damages.—

"(1) Determination of punitive damages.—A complaining party may recover punitive damages under this section against a respondent (other than a government, government agency or political subdivision) if the complaining party demonstrates that the respondent engaged in a discriminatory practice or discriminatory practices with malice or with reckless indifference to the federally protected rights of an aggrieved individual.

"(2) Exclusions from compensatory damages.—Compensatory damages awarded under this section shall not include backpay, interest on backpay, or any other type of relief authorized under section 706(g) of the Civil Rights Act of 1964.

"(3) Limitations.—The sum of the amount of compensatory damages awarded under this section for future pecuniary losses, emotional pain, suffering, inconvenience, mental anguish, loss of enjoyment of life, and other nonpecuniary losses, and the amount of punitive damages awarded under this section, shall not exceed, for each complaining party—

"(A) in the case of a respondent who has more than 14 and fewer than 101 employees in each of 20 or more calendar weeks in the current or preceding calendar year, $50,000;

"(B) in the case of a respondent who has more than 100 and fewer than 201 employees in each of 20 or more calendar weeks in the current or preceding calendar year, $100,000; and

"(C) in the case of a respondent who has more than 200 and fewer than 501 employees in each of 20 or more calendar weeks in the current or preceding calendar year, $200,000; and

"(D) in the case of a respondent who has more than 500 employees in each of 20 or more calendar weeks in the current or preceding calendar year, $300,000.

"(4) Construction.—Nothing in this section shall be construed to limit the scope of, or the relief available under, section 1977 of the Revised Statutes (42 U.S.C. § 1981).

"(c) Jury Trial.—If a complaining party seeks compensatory or punitive damages under this section—-

"(1) any party may demand a trial by jury; and

"(2) the court shall not inform the jury of the limitations described in subsection (b)(3).

"(d) Definitions.—As used in this section:

"(1) Complaining party.—The term 'complaining party' means—

"(A) in the case of a person seeking to bring an action under subsection (a)(1), the Equal Employment Opportunity Commission, the Attorney General, or a person who may bring an action or proceeding under title VII of the Civil Rights Act of 1964 (42 U.S.C. § 2000e et seq.); or

"(B) in the case of a person seeking to bring an action under subsection (a)(2), the Equal Employment Opportunity Commission, the Attorney General, a person who may bring an action or proceeding under section 505(a)(1) of the Rehabilitation Act of 1973 (29 U.S.C. § 794a(a)(1)), or a person who may bring an action or proceeding under title I of the Americans with Disabilities Act of 1990 (42 U.S.C. § 12101 *et seq.).*

"(2) Discriminatory practice.—The term 'discriminatory practice' means the discrimination described in paragraph (1), or the discrimination or the violation described in paragraph (2), of subsection (a).

SECTION 103. ATTORNEY'S FEES

[This section amends section 722 of the Revised Statutes (42 U.S.C. § 1988) by adding a reference to section 102 of the Civil Rights Act of 1991 to the list of civil rights actions in which reasonable attorney's fees may be awarded to the prevailing party, other than the United States.]

SECTION 105. BURDEN OF PROOF IN DISPARATE IMPACT CASES

(a) [This subsection amends section 703 of the Civil Rights Act of 1964 (42 U.S.C. § 2000e-2) by adding a new subsection (k), on the burden of proof in disparate impact cases.]

SECTION 106. PROHIBITION AGAINST DISCRIMINATORY USE OF TEST SCORES

[This section amends section 703 of the Civil Rights Act of 1964 (42 U.S.C. § 2000e-2) by adding a new subsection (l), on the prohibition against discriminatory use of test scores.]

SECTION 107. CLARIFYING PROHIBITION AGAINST IMPERMISSIBLE CONSIDERATION OF RACE, COLOR, RELIGION, SEX, OR NATIONAL ORIGIN IN EMPLOYMENT PRACTICES

(a) In general. [This subsection amends section 703 of the Civil Rights Act of 1964 (42 U.S.C. § 2000e-2) by adding a new subsection (m), clarifying the prohibition against consideration of race, color, religion, sex, or national origin in employment practices.]

(b) Enforcement provisions. [This subsection amends section 706(g) of the Civil Rights Act of 1964 (42 U.S.C. § 2000e-5(g)) by renumbering existing subsection (g), and adding at the end a new subparagraph (B) to provide a limitation on available relief in "mixed motive" cases (where the employer demonstrates it would have made the same decision in the absence of discrimination).]

SECTION 109. PROTECTION OF EXTRATERRITORIAL EMPLOYMENT

(a) Definition of Employee. [This subsection amends the definition of "employee" in section 701(f) of the Civil Rights Act of 1964 (42 U.S.C. § 2000e(f)) and section 101(4) of the Americans with Disabilities Act of 1990 (42 U.S.C. § 12111(4)) by adding a sentence to the end of each definition to include U.S. citizens employed abroad within the laws' protections.]

SECTION 112. EXPANSION OF RIGHT TO CHALLENGE DISCRIMINATORY SENIORITY SYSTEMS

[This section amends section 706(e) of the Civil Rights Act of 1964 (42 U.S.C. § 2000e-5(e)) by renumbering the subsection and adding at the end a paragraph to expand the right of claimants to challenge discriminatory seniority systems.]

SECTION 113. AUTHORIZING AWARD OF EXPERT FEES

(b) Civil Rights Act of 1964. [This section amends section 706(k) of the Civil Rights Act of 1964 (42 U.S.C. § 2000e-5(k)) to provide for recovery of expert fees as part of an attorney's fees award.]

SECTION 114. PROVIDING FOR INTEREST AND EXTENDING THE STATUTE OF LIMITATIONS IN ACTIONS AGAINST THE FEDERAL GOVERNMENT

[This section amends section 717 of the Civil Rights Act of 1964 (42 U.S.C. § 2000e-16) by extending the time for federal employees or applicants to file a civil action from 30 to 90 days (from receipt of notice of final action taken by a department, agency or unit), and allowing federal employees or applicants the same interest to compensate for delay in payments as is available in cases involving nonpublic parties.]

SECTION 116. LAWFUL, COURT-ORDERED REMEDIES, AFFIRMATIVE ACTION, AND CONCILIATION AGREEMENTS NOT AFFECTED

Nothing in the amendments made by this title shall be construed to affect court-ordered remedies, affirmative action, or conciliation agreements, that are in accordance with the law.

SECTION 117. COVERAGE OF HOUSE OF REPRESENTATIVES AND THE AGENCIES OF THE LEGISLATIVE BRANCH

(a) Coverage of the House of Representatives. [This subsection extends the rights and protections of Title VII of the Civil Rights Act of 1964, as amended, to employees of the U.S. House of Representatives. Procedures for processing discrimination complaints are handled internally by the House, not by the EEOC.] [2 U.S.C. § 60l]

(b) Instrumentalities of Congress. [This subsection extends the rights and protections of the Civil Rights Act of 1991 and Title VII of the Civil Rights Act of 1964, as amended, to "Instrumentalities of Congress," which are defined to include: the Architect of the Capitol, the Congressional Budget Office, the General Accounting Office, the Government Printing Office, the Office of Technology Assessment, and the United States Botanic Garden. Each agency is to establish its own remedies and procedures for enforcement.]

SECTION 118. ALTERNATIVE MEANS OF DISPUTE RESOLUTION

Where appropriate and to the extent authorized by law, the use of alternative means of dispute resolution, including settlement negotiations, conciliation, facilitation, mediation, factfinding, minitrials, and arbitration, is encouraged to resolve disputes arising under the Acts or provisions of Federal law amended by this title.

TITLE III—GOVERNMENT EMPLOYEE RIGHTS

SECTION 301. [2 U.S.C. § 1201]. GOVERNMENT EMPLOYEE RIGHTS ACT OF 1991

(a) Short title.—This title may be cited as the "Government Employee Rights Act of 1991".

(b) Purpose.—The purpose of this title is to provide procedures to protect the right of Senate and other government employees, with respect to their public employment, to be free of discrimination on the basis of race, color, religion, sex, national origin, age, or disability.

SECTION 302. [2 U.S.C. § 1202]. DISCRIMINATORY PRACTICES PROHIBITED

[Sections 320 and 321 (which protect Presidential appointees and previously exempt state employees who may file complaints of discrimination with EEOC under this title) refer to the rights, protections and remedies of this section and section 307(h).]

All personnel actions affecting employees of the Senate shall be made free from any discrimination based on—

(1) race, color, religion, sex, or national origin, within the meaning of section 717 of the Civil Rights Act of 1964 (42 U.S.C. § 2000E-16) . . .

APPENDIX 4: SELECTED PROVISIONS - THE EQUAL PAY ACT OF 1963

An Act:

To prohibit discrimination on account of sex in the payment of wages by employers engaged in commerce or in the production of goods for commerce.

Be it enacted by the Senate and House of Representatives of the United States of America in Congress assembled, That this Act may be cited as the "Equal Pay Act of 1963."

PURPOSE

(a) The Congress hereby finds that the existence in industries engaged in commerce or in the production of goods for commerce of wage differentials based on sex—

(1) depresses wages and living standards for employees necessary for their health and efficiency;

(2) prevents the maximum utilization of the available labor resources;

(3) tends to cause labor disputes, thereby burdening, affecting, and obstructing commerce;

(4) burdens commerce and the free flow of goods in commerce; and

(5) constitutes an unfair method of competition.

(b) It is hereby declared to be the policy of this Act, through exercise by Congress of its power to regulate commerce among the several States and with foreign nations, to correct the conditions above referred to in such industries.

* * *

SECTION 206. MINIMUM WAGE

(d) (1) No employer having employees subject to any provisions of this section shall discriminate, within any establishment in which such employees are employed, between employees on the basis of sex by paying wages to employees in such establishment at a rate less than the rate at which he pays wages to employees of the opposite sex in such establishment for equal work on jobs the performance of which requires equal skill, effort, and responsibility, and which are performed under similar working conditions, except where such payment is made pursuant to (i) a seniority system; (ii) a merit system; (iii) a system which measures earnings by quantity or quality of production; or (iv) a differential based on any other factor other than sex: Provided, That an employer who is paying a wage rate differential in violation of this subsection shall not, in order to comply with the provisions of this subsection, reduce the wage rate of any employee.

(2) No labor organization, or its agents, representing employees of an employer having employees subject to any provisions of this section shall cause or attempt to cause such an employer to discriminate against an employee in violation of paragraph (1) of this subsection.

(3) For purposes of administration and enforcement, any amounts owing to any employee which have been withheld in violation of this subsection shall be deemed to be unpaid minimum wages or unpaid overtime compensation under this chapter.

(4) As used in this subsection, the term "labor organization" means any organization of any kind, or any agency or employee representation committee or plan, in which employees participate and which exists for the purpose, in whole or in part, of dealing with employers concerning grievances, labor disputes, wages, rates of pay, hours of employment, or conditions of work.

* * *

SECTION 209. ATTENDANCE OF WITNESSES

For the purpose of any hearing or investigation provided for in this chapter, the provisions of sections 49 and 50 of title 15 *[sections 9 and 10]* (relating to the attendance of witnesses and the production of books, papers, and documents), of the Federal Trade Commission Act of September 16, 1914, as amended (U.S.C., 1934 edition, title 15, secs. 4

and 50), are made applicable to the jurisdiction, powers, and duties of the Administrator, the Secretary of Labor, and the industry committees.

* * *

SECTION 211. INVESTIGATIONS, INSPECTIONS, RECORDS, AND HOMEWORK REGULATIONS

(a) The Administrator or his designated representatives may investigate and gather data regarding the wages, hours, and other conditions and practices of employment in any industry subject to this chapter, and may enter and inspect such places and such records (and make such transcriptions thereof), question such employees, and investigate such facts, conditions, practices, or matters as he may deem necessary or appropriate to determine whether any person has violated any provision of this chapter, or which may aid in the enforcement of the provisions of this chapter. Except as provided in section 212 *[section 12]* of this title and in subsection (b) of this section, the Administrator shall utilize the bureaus and divisions of the Department of Labor for all the investigations and inspections necessary under this section. Except as provided in section 212 *[section 12]*, the Administrator shall bring all actions under section 217 *[section 17]* of this title to restrain violations of this chapter.

(b) With the consent and cooperation of State agencies charged with the administration of State labor laws, the Administrator and the Secretary of Labor may, for the purpose of carrying out their respective functions and duties under this chapter, utilize the services of State and local agencies and their employees and, notwithstanding any other provision of law, may reimburse such State and local agencies and their employees for services rendered for such purposes.

(c) Every employer subject to any provision of this chapter or of any order issued under this chapter shall make, keep, and preserve such records of the persons employed by him and of the wages, hours, and other conditions and practices of employment maintained by him, and shall preserve such records for such periods of time, and shall make such reports therefrom to the Administrator as he shall prescribe by regulation or order as necessary or appropriate for the enforcement of the provisions of this chapter or the regulations or orders thereunder. The employer of an employee who performs substitute work described in section 207(p)(3) *[section 7(p)(3)]* of this title may not be required under this subsection to keep a record of the hours of the substitute work.

(d) The Administrator is authorized to make such regulations and orders regulating, restricting, or prohibiting industrial homework as are necessary or appropriate to prevent the circumvention or evasion of and to safeguard the minimum wage rate prescribed in this chapter, and all existing regulations or orders of the Administrator relating to industrial homework are continued in full force and effect.

* * *

SECTION 213. EXEMPTIONS

(a) The provisions of sections 206 *[section 6]* (except subsection (d) in the case of paragraph (1) of this subsection) and section 207 *[section 7]* shall not apply with respect to-

(1) any employee employed in a bona fide executive, administrative, or professional capacity (including any employee employed in the capacity of academic administrative personnel or teacher in elementary or secondary schools), or in the capacity of outside salesman (as such terms are defined and delimited from time to time by regulations of the Secretary, subject to the provisions of subchapter II of chapter 5 of title 5 *[the Administrative Procedure Act]*, except that an employee of a retail or service establishment shall not be excluded from the definition of employee employed in a bona fide executive or administrative capacity because of the number of hours in his workweek which he devotes to activities not directly or closely related to the performance of executive or administrative activities, if less than 40 per centum of his hours worked in the workweek are devoted to such activities); or

(2) *** (Repealed)

[Note: Section 13(a)(2) (relating to employees employed by a retail or service establishment) was repealed by Pub. L. 101-157, section 3(c)(1), November 17, 1989.]

(3) any employee employed by an establishment which is an amusement or recreational establishment, organized camp, or religious or non-profit educational conference center, if (A) it does not operate for more than seven months in any calendar year, or (B) during the preceding calendar year, its average receipts for any six months of such year were not more than 33 1/3 per centum of its average receipts for the other six months of such year, except that the exemption from sections 206 and 207 *[sections 6 and 7]* of this title provided by this paragraph does not apply with respect to any employee of a private entity engaged in providing services or facilities (other than, in the case of the exemption from section 206 *[section 6]*, a private entity engaged in providing services and facilities directly related to skiing) in a national park or a national forest, or on land in the National Wildlife Refuge System, under a contract with the Secretary of the Interior or the Secretary of Agriculture; or

(4) *** (Repealed)

[Note: Section 13(a)(4) (relating to employees employed by an establishment which qualified as an exempt retail establishment) was repealed by Pub. L. 101-157, Section 3(c)(1), November 17, 1989.]

(5) any employee employed in the catching, taking, propagating, harvesting, cultivating, or farming of any kind of fish, shellfish, crustacea, sponges, seaweeds, or other aquatic forms of animal and vegetable life, or in the first processing, canning or packing such marine products at sea as an incident to, or in conjunction with, such fishing operations, including the going to and returning from work and loading and unloading when performed by any such employee; or

(6) any employee employed in agriculture (A) if such employee is employed by an employer who did not, during any calendar quarter during the preceding calendar year, use more than five hundred man-days or agricultural labor, (B) if such employee is the parent, spouse, child, or other member of his employer's immediate family, (C) if such employee (i) is employed as a hand harvest laborer and is paid on a piece rate basis in an operation which has been, and is customarily and generally recognized as having been, paid on a piece rate basis in the region of employment, (ii) commutes daily from his permanent residence to the farm on which he is so employed, and (iii) has been employed in agriculture less than thirteen weeks during the preceding calendar year, (D) if such employee (other than an employee described in clause (C) of this subsection) (i) is sixteen years of age or under and is employed as a hand harvest laborer, is paid on a piece rate basis in an operation which has been, and is customarily and generally recognized as having been, paid on a piece rate basis in the region of employment, (ii) is employed on the same farm as his parent or person standing in the place of his parent, and (iii) is paid at the same piece rate as employees over age sixteen are paid on the same farm, or (E) if such employee is principally engaged in the range production of livestock; or

(7) any employee to the extent that such employee is exempted by regulations, order, or certificate of the Secretary issued under section 214 *[section 14]* of this title; or

(8) any employee employed in connection with the publication of any weekly, semiweekly, or daily newspaper with a circulation of

less than four thousand the major part of which circulation is within the county where published or counties contiguous thereto; or

(9) *** (Repealed)

[Note: Section 13(a)(9) (relating to motion picture theater employees) was repealed by section 23 of the Fair Labor Standards Amendments of 1974. The 1974 amendments created an exemption for such employees from the overtime provisions only in section 13(b)27.]

(10) any switchboard operator employed by an independently owned public telephone company which has not more than seven hundred and fifty stations; or

(11) *** (Repealed)

[Note: Section 13(a)(11) (relating to telegraph agency employees) was repealed by section 10 of the Fair Labor Standards Amendments of 1974. The 1974 amendments created an exemption from the overtime provisions only in section 13(b)(23), which was repealed effective May 1, 1976.]

(12) any employee employed as a seaman on a vessel other than an American vessel; or

(13) *** (Repealed)

[Note: Section 13(a)(13) (relating to small logging crews) was repealed by section 23 of the Fair Labor Standards Amendments of 1974. The 1974 amendments created an exemption for such employees from the overtime provisions only in section 13(b)(28)]

(14) *** (Repealed)

[Note: Section 13(a)(14) (relating to employees employed in growing and harvesting of shade grown tobacco) was repealed by section 9 of the Fair Labor Standards Amendments of 1974. The 1974 amendments created an exemption for certain tobacco producing employees from the overtime provisions only in section 13(b)(22). The section 13(b)(22) exemption was repealed, effective January 1, 1978, by section 5 of the Fair Labor Standards Amendments of 1977.]

(15) any employee employed on a casual basis in domestic service employment to provide babysitting services or any employee employed in domestic service employment to provide companionship services for individuals who (because of age or infirmity) are unable to care for themselves (as such terms are defined and delimited by regulations of the Secretary).

(g) The exemption from section 206 *[section 6]* of this title provided by paragraph (6) of subsection (a) of this section shall not apply with respect to any employee employed by an establishment (1) which controls, is controlled by, or is under common control with, another establishment the activities of which are not related for a common business purpose to, but materially support the activities of the establishment employing such employee; and (2) whose annual gross volume of sales made or business done, when combined with the annual gross volume of sales made or business done by each establishment which controls, is controlled by, or is under common control with, the establishment employing such employee, exceeds $10,000,000 (exclusive of excise taxes at the retail level which are separately stated).

* * *

SECTION 215. PROHIBITED ACTS

(a) After the expiration of one hundred and twenty days from June 25, 1938 [the date of enactment of this Act], it shall be unlawful for any person—

(1) to transport, offer for transportation, ship, deliver, or sell in commerce, or to ship, deliver, or sell with knowledge that shipment or delivery or sale thereof in commerce is intended, any goods in the production of which any employee was employed in violation of section 206 or section 207 of this title, or in violation of any regulation or order of the Secretary issued under section 214 of this title . . .

(2) to violate any of the provisions of section 206 or section 207 of this title, on any of the provisions of any regulation or order of the Secretary issued under section 214 of this title;

(3) to discharge or in any other manner discriminate against any employee because such employee has filed any complaint or instituted or caused to be instituted any proceeding under or related to this chapter, or has testified or is about to testify in any such proceeding, or has served or is about to serve on an industry committee;

(4) to violate any of the provisions of section 212 of this title;

(5) to violate any of the provisions of section 211(c) of this title, or any regulation or order made or continued in effect under the provisions of section 211(d) of this title, or to make any statement, report, or record filed or kept pursuant to the provisions of such section or of any regulation or order thereunder, knowing such statement, report, or record to be false in a material respect.

(b) For the purpose of subsection (a)(1) of this section proof that any employee was employed in any place of employment where goods shipped or sold in commerce were produced, within ninety days prior to the removal of the goods from such place of employment, shall be *prima facie* evidence that such employee was engaged in the production of such goods.

SECTION 216. PENALTIES

(a) Any person who willfully violates any of the provisions of section 215 [section 15] of this title shall upon conviction thereof be subject to a fine of not more than $10,000, or to imprisonment for not more than six months, or both. No person shall be imprisoned under this subsection except for an offense committed after the conviction of such person for a prior offense under this subsection.

(b) Any employer who violates the provisions of section 206 or section 207 of this title shall be liable to the employee or employees affected in the amount of their unpaid minimum wages, or their unpaid overtime compensation, as the case may be, and in an additional equal amount as liquidated damages. Any employer who violates the provisions of section 215(a)(3) [section 15(a)(3)] of this title shall be liable for such legal or equitable relief as may be appropriate to effectuate the purposes of section 215(a)(3) [section 15(a)(3)], including without limitation employment, reinstatement, promotion, and the payment of wages lost and an additional equal amount as liquidated damages. An action to recover the liability prescribed in either of the preceding sentences may be maintained against any employer (including a public agency) in an Federal or State court of competent jurisdiction by any one or more employees for and in behalf of himself or themselves and other employees similarly situated. No employee shall be a party plaintiff to any such action unless he gives his consent in writing to become such a party and such consent is filed in the court in which such action is brought. The court in such action shall, in addition to any judgment awarded to the plaintiff or plaintiffs, allow a reasonable attorney's fee to be paid by the defendant, and costs of the action. The right provided by this subsection to bring an action by or on behalf of any employee, and the right of any employee to become a party plaintiff to any such action, shall terminate upon the filing of a complaint by the Secretary of Labor in an action under section 217 in which (1) restraint is sought of any further delay in the payment of unpaid minimum wages, or the amount of unpaid overtime compensation as the case may be, owing to such employee under section 206 or section 207 of this title by an employer liable therefore under the provisions of this subsection or

(2) legal or equitable relief is sought as a result of alleged violations of section 215(a)(3) of this title.

(c) The Secretary is authorized to supervise the payment of the unpaid minimum wages or the unpaid overtime compensation owing to any employee or employees under section 206 *[section 6]* or section 207 *[section 7]* of this title, and the agreement of any employee to accept such payment shall upon payment in full constitute a waiver by such employee of any right he may have under subsection (b) of this section to such unpaid minimum wages or unpaid overtime compensation and an additional equal amount as liquidated damages. The Secretary may bring an action in any court of competent jurisdiction to recover the amount of the unpaid minimum wages or overtime compensation and an equal amount as liquidated damages. The right provided by subsection (b) to bring an action by or on behalf of any employee to recover the liability specified in the first sentence of such subsection and of any employee to become a party plaintiff to any such action shall terminate upon the filing of a complaint by the Secretary in an action under this subsection in which a recovery is sought of unpaid minimum wages or unpaid overtime compensation under sections 206 and 207 *[sections 6 and 7]* of this title or liquidated or other damages provided by this subsection owing to suchemployee by an employer liable under the provisions of subsection (b) of this section, unless such action is dismissed without prejudice on motion of the Secretary. Any sums thus recovered by the Secretary of Labor on behalf of an employee pursuant to this subsection shall be held in a special deposit account and shall be paid on order of the Secretary of Labor, directly to the employee or employees affected. Any such sums not paid to an employee because of inability to do so within a period of three years shall be covered into the Treasury of the United States as miscellaneous receipts. In determining when an action is commenced by the Secretary of Labor under this subsection for the purposes of the statutes of limitations provided in section 255(a) of this title *[section 6(a) of the Portal-to-Portal Act of 1947]*, it shall be considered to be commenced in the case of any individual claimant on the date when the complaint is filed if he is specifically named as a party plaintiff in the complaint, or if his name did not so appear, on the subsequent date on which his name is added as a party plaintiff in such action.

(d) In any action or proceeding commenced prior to, on, or after August 8, 1956 *[the date of enactment of this subsection]*, no employer shall be subject to any liability or punishment under this chapter or the Portal-to-Portal Act of 1947 *[29 U.S.C. 251 et seq.]* or on account of his failure to comply with any provision or provisions or such Act (1) with respect to work heretofore or hereafter performed in a work place to which the exemption in section 213(f) *[section 13(f)]* is applicable, (2) with respect to work performed in Guam, the Canal Zone or Wake Island before the effective date of this amendment of subsection (d), or (3) with respect to work performed in a possession named in section 206(a)(3) *[section 6(a)(3)]* of this title at any time prior to the establishment by the Secretary, as provided therein, of a minimum wage rate applicable to such work.

(e) Any person who violates the provisions of section 212 of this title, relating to child labor, or any regulation issued under that section, shall be subject to a civil penalty of not to exceed $10,000 for each employee who was the subject of such a violation. Any person who repeatedly or willfully violates section 206 or 207 of this title shall be subject to a civil penalty of not to exceed $1,000 for each such violation. In determining the amount of any penalty under this subsection, the appropriateness of such penalty to the size of the business of the person charged and the gravity of the violation shall be considered. The amount of any penalty under this subsection, when finally determined, may be-

(1) deducted from any sums owing by the United States to the person charged;

(2) recovered in a civil action brought by the Secretary in any court of competent jurisdiction, in which litigation the Secretary shall be represented by the Solicitor of Labor; or

(3) ordered by the court, in an action brought for a violation of section 215(a)(4) of this title or a repeated or willful violation of section 215(a)(2) of this title, to be paid to the Secretary.

Any administrative determination by the Secretary of the amount of any penalty under this subsection shall be final, unless within fifteen days after receipt of notice thereof by certified mail the person charged with the violation takes exception to the determination that the violations for which the penalty is imposed occurred, in which event final determination of the penalty shall be made in an administrative proceeding after opportunity for hearing in accordance with section 554 of Title 5, and regulations to be promulgated by the Secretary. Except for civil penalties collected for violations of section 212 of this title, sums collected as penalties pursuant to this section shall be applied toward reimbursement of the costs of determining the violations and assessing and collecting such penalties, in accordance with the provisions of section 9a of this title. Civil penalties collected for violations of section 212 of this title shall be deposited in the general fund of the Treasury.

SECTION 217. INJUNCTION PROCEEDINGS

The districts courts, together with the United States District Court for the District of the Canal Zone, the District Court of the Virgin Islands, and the District Court of Guam shall have jurisdiction, for cause shown, to restrain violations of section 215 *[section 15]* of this title, including in the case of violations of section 15(a)(2) of this title the restraint of any withholding of payment of minimum wages or overtime compensation found by the court to be due to employees under this chapter (except sums which employees are barred from recovering, at the time of the commencement of the action to restrain the violations, by virtue of the provisions of section 255 of this title *[section 6 of the Portal-to-Portal Act of 1947]*.

SECTION 218. RELATION TO OTHER LAWS

(a) No provision of this chapter or of any order thereunder shall excuse noncompliance with any Federal or State law or municipal ordinance establishing a minimum wage higher than the minimum wage established under this chapter or a maximum workweek lower than the maximum workweek established under this chapter, and no provision of this chapter relating to the employment of child labor shall justify noncompliance with any Federal or State law or municipal ordinance establishing a higher standard than the standard established under this chapter. No provision of this chapter shall justify any employer in reducing a wage paid by him which is in excess of the applicable minimum wage under this chapter, or justify any employer in increasing hours of employment maintained by him which are shorter than the maximum hours applicable under this chapter.

SECTION 219. SEPARABILITY OF PROVISIONS

If any provision of this chapter or the application of such provision to any person or circumstances is held invalid, the remainder of the chapter and the application of such provision to other persons or circumstances shall not be affected thereby.

APPENDIX 5: SELECTED PROVISIONS - THE AGE DISCRIMINATION IN EMPLOYMENT ACT (ADEA) OF 1967

An Act:

To prohibit age discrimination in employment.

Be it enacted by the Senate and House of Representatives of the United States of America in Congress assembled, that this Act may be cited as the "Age Discrimination in Employment Act of 1967".

SECTION 621. STATEMENT OF FINDINGS AND PURPOSE

(a) The Congress hereby finds and declares that-

(1) in the face of rising productivity and affluence, older workers find themselves disadvantaged in their efforts to retain employment, and especially to regain employment when displaced from jobs;

(2) the setting of arbitrary age limits regardless of potential for job performance has become a common practice, and certain otherwise desirable practices may work to the disadvantage of older persons;

(3) the incidence of unemployment, especially long-term unemployment with resultant deterioration of skill, morale, and employer acceptability is, relative to the younger ages, high among older workers; their numbers are great and growing; and their employment problems grave;

(4) the existence in industries affecting commerce, of arbitrary discrimination in employment because of age, burdens commerce and the free flow of goods in commerce.

(b) It is therefore the purpose of this chapter to promote employment of older persons based on their ability rather than age; to prohibit arbitrary age discrimination in employment; to help employers and workers find ways of meeting problems arising from the impact of age on employment.

* * *

SECTION 623. PROHIBITION OF AGE DISCRIMINATION

(a) It shall be unlawful for an employer-

(1) to fail or refuse to hire or to discharge any individual or otherwise discriminate against any individual with respect to his compensation, terms, conditions, or privileges of employment, because of such individual's age;

(2) to limit, segregate, or classify his employees in any way which would deprive or tend to deprive any individual of employment opportunities or otherwise adversely affect his status as an employee, because of such individual's age; or

(3) to reduce the wage rate of any employee in order to comply with this chapter.

(b) It shall be unlawful for an employment agency to fail or refuse to refer for employment, or otherwise to discriminate against, any individual because of such individual's age, or to classify or refer for employment any individual on the basis of such individual's age.

(c) It shall be unlawful for a labor organization-

(1) to exclude or to expel from its membership, or otherwise to discriminate against, any individual because of his age;

(2) to limit, segregate, or classify its membership, or to classify or fail or refuse to refer for employment any individual, in any way which would deprive or tend to deprive any individual of employment opportunities, or would limit such employment opportunities or otherwise adversely affect his status as an employee or as an applicant for employment, because of such individual's age;

(3) to cause or attempt to cause an employer to discriminate against an individual in violation of this section.

(d) It shall be unlawful for an employer to discriminate against any of his employees or applicants for employment, for an employment agency to discriminate against any individual, or for a labor organization to discriminate against any member thereof or applicant for membership, because such individual, member or applicant for membership has opposed any practice made unlawful by this section, or because such individual, member or applicant for membership has made a charge, testified, assisted, or participated in any manner in an investigation, proceeding, or litigation under this chapter.

(e) It shall be unlawful for an employer, labor organization, or employment agency to print or publish, or cause to be printed or published, any notice or advertisement relating to employment by such an employer or membership in or any classification or referral for employment by such a labor organization, or relating to any classification or referral for employment by such an employment agency, indicating any preference, limitation, specification, or discrimination, based on age.

(f) It shall not be unlawful for an employer, employment agency, or labor organization-

(1) to take any action otherwise prohibited under subsections (a), (b), (c), or (e) of this section where age is a bona fide occupational qualification reasonably necessary to the normal operation of the particular business, or where the differentiation is based on reasonable factors other than age, or where such practices involve an employee in a workplace in a foreign country, and compliance with such subsections would cause such employer, or a corporation controlled by such employer, to violate the laws of the country in which such workplace is located;

(2) to take any action otherwise prohibited under subsection (a), (b), (c), or (e) of this section-

(A) to observe the terms of a bona fide seniority system that is not intended to evade the purposes of this chapter, except that no such seniority system shall require or permit the involuntary retirement of any individual specified by section 631(a) of this title because of the age of such individual; or

(B) to observe the terms of a bona fide employee benefit plan-

(i) where, for each benefit or benefit package, the actual amount of payment made or cost incurred on behalf of an older worker is no less than that made or incurred on behalf of a younger worker, as permissible under section 1625.10, title 29, Code of Federal Regulations (as in effect on June 22, 1989); or

(ii) that is a voluntary early retirement incentive plan consistent with the relevant purpose or purposes of this chapter. Notwithstanding clause (i) or (ii) of subparagraph (B), no such employee benefit plan or voluntary early retirement incentive plan shall excuse the failure to hire any individual, and no such employee benefit plan shall require or permit the involuntary retirement of any individual specified by section 631(a) of this title, because of the age of such individual. An employer, employment agency, or labor organization acting under subparagraph (A), or under clause (i) or (ii) of subparagraph (B), shall have the burden of proving that such actions are lawful in any civil enforcement proceeding brought under this chapter; or

(3) to discharge or otherwise discipline an individual for good cause.

(g) [Repealed]

(h) (1) If an employer controls a corporation whose place of incorporation is in a foreign country, any practice by such corporation prohibited under this section shall be presumed to be such practice by such employer.

(2) The prohibitions of this section shall not apply where the employer is a foreign person not controlled by an American employer.

(3) For the purpose of this subsection the determination of whether an employer controls a corporation shall be based upon the-

(A) interrelation of operations,

(B) common management,

(C) centralized control of labor relations, and

(D) common ownership or financial control, of the employer and the corporation.

(i) It shall not be unlawful for an employer which is a State, a political subdivision of a State, an agency or instrumentality of a State or a political subdivision of a State, or an interstate agency to fail or refuse to hire or to discharge any individual because of such individual's age if such action is taken-

(1) with respect to the employment of an individual as a firefighter or as a law enforcement officer and the individual has attained the age of hiring or retirement in effect under applicable State or local law on March 3, 1983, and

(2) pursuant to a bona fide hiring or retirement plan that is not a subterfuge to evade the purposes of this chapter.

(j) (1) Except as otherwise provided in this subsection, it shall be unlawful for an employer, an employment agency, a labor organization, or any combination thereof to establish or maintain an employee pension benefit plan which requires or permits-

(A) in the case of a defined benefit plan, the cessation of an employee's benefit accrual, or the reduction of the rate of an employee's benefit accrual, because of age, or

(B) in the case of a defined contribution plan, the cessation of allocations to an employee's account, or the reduction of the rate at which amounts are allocated to an employee's account, because of age.

(2) Nothing in this section shall be construed to prohibit an employer, employment agency, or labor organization from observing any provision of an employee pension benefit plan to the extent that such provision imposes (without regard to age) a limitation on the amount of benefits that the plan provides or a limitation on the number of years of service or years of participation which are taken into account for purposes of determining benefit accrual under the plan.

(3) In the case of any employee who, as of the end of any plan year under a defined benefit plan, has attained normal retirement age under such plan-

(A) if distribution of benefits under such plan with respect to such employee has commenced as of the end of such plan year, then any requirement of this subsection for continued accrual of benefits under such plan with respect to such employee during such plan year shall be treated as satisfied to the extent of the actuarial equivalent of in-service distribution of benefits, and

(B) if distribution of benefits under such plan with respect to such employee has not commenced as of the end of such year in accordance with section 1056(a)(3) of this title [section 206(a)(3) of the Employee Retirement Income Security Act of 1974] and section 401(a)(14)(C) of title 26 [the Internal Revenue Code of 1986], and the payment of benefits under such plan with respect to such employee is not suspended during such plan year pursuant to section 1053(a)(3)(B) of this title [section 203(a)(3)(B) of the Employee Retirement Income Security Act of 1974] or section 411(a)(3)(B) of title 26 [the Internal Revenue Code of 1986], then any requirement of this subsection for continued accrual of benefits under such plan with respect to such employee during such plan year shall be treated as satisfied to the extent of any adjustment in the benefit payable under the plan during such plan year attributable to the delay in the distribution of benefits after the attainment of normal retirement age.

The provisions of this paragraph shall apply in accordance with regulations of the Secretary of the Treasury. Such regulations shall provide for the application of the preceding provisions of this paragraph to all employee pension benefit plans subject to this subsection and may provide for the application of such provisions, in the case of any such employee, with respect to any period of time within a plan year.

(4) Compliance with the requirements of this subsection with respect to an employee pension benefit plan shall constitute compliance with the requirements of this section relating to benefit accrual under such plan.

(5) Paragraph (1) shall not apply with respect to any employee who is a highly compensated employee (within the meaning of section 414(q) of title 26 [the Internal Revenue Code of 1986]) to the extent provided in regulations prescribed by the Secretary of the Treasury for purposes of precluding discrimination in favor of highly compensated employees within the meaning of subchapter D of chapter 1 of title 26 [the Internal Revenue Code of 1986].

(6) A plan shall not be treated as failing to meet the requirements of paragraph (1) solely because the subsidized portion of any early retirement benefit is disregarded in determining benefit accruals.

(7) Any regulations prescribed by the Secretary of the Treasury pursuant to clause (v) of section 411(b)(1)(H) of title 26 [the Internal Revenue Code of 1986] and subparagraphs (C) and (D) of section 411(b)(2) of title 26 [the Internal Revenue Code of 1986] shall apply with respect to the requirements of this subsection in the same manner and to the same extent as such regulations apply with respect to the requirements of such sections 411(b)(1)(H) and 411(b)(2).

(8) A plan shall not be treated as failing to meet the requirements of this section solely because such plan provides a normal retirement age described in section 1002(24)(B) of this title [section 3(24)(B) of the Employee Retirement Income Security Act of 1974] and section 411(a)(8)(B) of title 26 [the Internal Revenue Code of 1986].

(9) For purposes of this subsection-

(A) The terms "employee pension benefit plan", "defined benefit plan", "defined contribution plan", and "normal retirement age" have the meanings provided such terms in section 1002 of this title [section 3 of the Employee Retirement Income Security Act of 1974].

(B) The term "compensation" has the meaning provided by section 414(s) of title 26 [the Internal Revenue Code of 1986].

(k) A seniority system or employee benefit plan shall comply with this chapter regardless of the date of adoption of such system or plan.

(l) Notwithstanding clause (i) or (ii) of subsection (f)(2)(B) of this section-

(1) It shall not be a violation of subsection (a), (b), (c), or (e) of this section solely because-

(A) an employee pension benefit plan (as defined in section 1002(2) of this title [section 3(2) of the Employee Retirement Income Security Act of 1974]) provides for the attainment of a minimum age as a condition of eligibility for normal or early retirement benefits; or

(B) a defined benefit plan (as defined in section 1002(35) of this title [section 3(35) of such Act]) provides for-

(i) payments that constitute the subsidized portion of an early retirement benefit; or

(ii) social security supplements for plan participants that commence before the age and terminate at the age (specified by the plan) when participants are eligible to receive reduced or unreduced old-age insurance benefits under title II of the Social Security Act (42 U.S.C. 401 et seq.), and that do not exceed such old-age insurance benefits.

(2) (A) It shall not be a violation of subsection (a), (b), (c), or (e) of this section solely because following a contingent event unrelated to age

(i) the value of any retiree health benefits received by an individual eligible for an immediate pension;

(ii) the value of any additional pension benefits that are made available solely as a result of the contingent event unrelated to age and following which the individual is eligible for not less than an immediate and unreduced pension; or

(iii) the values described in both clauses (i) and (ii); are deducted from severance pay made available as a result of the contingent event unrelated to age.

(B) For an individual who receives immediate pension benefits that are actuarially reduced under subparagraph (A)(i), the amount of the deduction available pursuant to subparagraph (A)(i) shall be reduced by the same percentage as the reduction in the pension benefits.

(C) For purposes of this paragraph, severance pay shall include that portion of supplemental unemployment compensation benefits (as described in section 501(c)(17) of title 26 [the Internal Revenue Code of 1986]) that-

(i) constitutes additional benefits of up to 52 weeks;

(ii) has the primary purpose and effect of continuing benefits until an individual becomes eligible for an immediate and unreduced pension; and

(iii) is discontinued once the individual becomes eligible for an immediate and unreduced pension.

(D) For purposes of this paragraph and solely in order to make the deduction authorized under this paragraph, the term "retiree health benefits" means benefits provided pursuant to a group health plan covering retirees, for which (determined as of the contingent event unrelated to age)-

(i) the package of benefits provided by the employer for the retirees who are below age 65 is at least comparable to benefits provided under title XVIII of the Social Security Act (42 U.S.C. 1395 et seq.);

(ii) the package of benefits provided by the employer for the retirees who are age 65 and above is at least comparable to that offered under a plan that provides a benefit package with one-fourth the value of benefits provided under title XVIII of such Act; or

(iii) the package of benefits provided by the employer is as described in clauses (i) and (ii).

(E) (i) If the obligation of the employer to provide retiree health benefits is of limited duration, the value for each individual shall be calculated at a rate of $3,000 per year for benefit years before age 65, and $750 per year for benefit years beginning at age 65 and above.

(ii) If the obligation of the employer to provide retiree health benefits is of unlimited duration, the value for each individual shall be calculated at a rate of $48,000 for individuals below age 65, and $24,000 for individuals age 65 and above.

(iii) The values described in clauses (i) and (ii) shall be calculated based on the age of the individual as of the date of the contingent event unrelated to age. The values are effective on October 16, 1990, and shall be adjusted on an annual basis, with respect to a contingent event that occurs subsequent to the first year after October 16, 1990, based on the medical component of the Consumer Price Index for all-urban consumers published by the Department of Labor.

(iv) If an individual is required to pay a premium for retiree health benefits, the value calculated pursuant to this subparagraph shall be reduced by whatever percentage of the overall premium the individual is required to pay.

(F) If an employer that has implemented a deduction pursuant to subparagraph (A) fails to fulfill the obligation described in subparagraph

(E), any aggrieved individual may bring an action for specific performance of the obligation described in subparagraph (E). The relief shall be in addition to any other remedies provided under Federal or State law.

(3) It shall not be a violation of subsection (a), (b), (c), or (e) of this section solely because an employer provides a bona fide employee benefit plan or plans under which long-term disability benefits received by an individual are reduced by any pension benefits (other than those attributable to employee contributions)-

(A) paid to the individual that the individual voluntarily elects to receive; or

(B) for which an individual who has attained the later of age 62 or normal retirement age is eligible.

* * *

SECTION 627. NOTICE TO BE POSTED

Every employer, employment agency, and labor organization shall post and keep posted in conspicuous places upon its premises a notice to be prepared or approved by the Equal Employment Opportunity Commission setting forth information as the Commission deems appropriate to effectuate the purposes of this chapter.

* * *

SECTION 629. CRIMINAL PENALTIES

Whoever shall forcibly resist, oppose, impede, intimidate or interfere with a duly authorized representative of the Equal Employment Opportunity Commission while it is engaged in the performance of duties under this chapter shall be punished by a fine of not more than $500 or by imprisonment for not more than one year, or by both: Provided, however, That no person shall be imprisoned under this section except when there has been a prior conviction hereunder.

* * *

SECTION 631. AGE LIMITATION

(a) The prohibitions in this chapter [except the provisions of section 4(g)] shall be limited to individuals who are at least 40 years of age.

(b) In the case of any personnel action affecting employees or applicants for employment which is subject to the provisions of section 633a of this title [section 15], the prohibitions established in section 633a of this title [section 15] shall be limited to individuals who are at least 40 years of age.

(c) (1) Nothing in this chapter shall be construed to prohibit compulsory retirement of any employee who has attained 65 years of age and who, for the 2-year period immediately before retirement, is employed in a bona fide executive or a high policymaking position, if such employee is entitled to an immediate nonforfeitable annual retirement benefit from a pension, profit-sharing, savings, or deferred compensation plan, or any combination of such plans, of the employer of such employee, which equals, in the aggregate, at least $44,000.

(2) In applying the retirement benefit test of paragraph (1) of this subsection, if any such retirement benefit is in a form other than a straight life annuity (with no ancillary benefits), or if employees contribute to any such plan or make rollover contributions, such benefit shall be adjusted in accordance with regulations prescribed by the Equal Employment Opportunity Commission, after consultation with the Secretary of the Treasury, so that the benefit is the equivalent of a straight life annuity (with no ancillary benefits) under a plan to which employees do not contribute and under which no rollover contributions are made.

(d) Nothing in this chapter shall be construed to prohibit compulsory retirement of any employee who has attained 70 years of age, and who is serving under a contract of unlimited tenure (or similar arrangement providing for unlimited tenure) at an institution of higher education (as defined by section 1141(a) of title 20 [section 1201(a) of the Higher Education Act of 1965]).

* * *

SECTION 633A. NONDISCRIMINATION ON ACCOUNT OF AGE IN FEDERAL GOVERNMENT EMPLOYMENT

(a) All personnel actions affecting employees or applicants for employment who are at least 40 years of age (except personnel actions with regard to aliens employed outside the limits of the United States) in military departments as defined in section 102 of title 5 [United States Code], in executive agencies as defined in section 105 of title 5 [United States Code] (including employees and applicants for employment who are paid from nonappropriated funds), in the United States Postal Service and the Postal Rate Commission, in those units in the government of the District of Columbia having positions in the competitive service, and in those units of the legislative and judicial branches of the Federal Government having positions in the competitive service, and in the Library of Congress shall be made free from any discrimination based on age.

(b) Except as otherwise provided in this subsection, the Equal Employment Opportunity Commission is authorized to enforce the provisions of subsection (a) of this section through appropriate remedies, including reinstatement or hiring of employees with or without backpay, as will effectuate the policies of this section. The Equal Employment Opportunity Commission shall issue such rules, regulations, orders, and instructions as it deems necessary and appropriate to carry out its responsibilities under this section. The Equal Employment Opportunity Commission shall-

(1) be responsible for the review and evaluation of the operation of all agency programs designed to carry out the policy of this section, periodically obtaining and publishing (on at least a semiannual basis) progress reports from each department, agency, or unit referred to in subsection (a) of this section;

(2) consult with and solicit the recommendations of interested individuals, groups, and organizations relating to nondiscrimination in employment on account of age; and

(3) provide for the acceptance and processing of complaints of discrimination in Federal employment on account of age.

The head of each such department, agency, or unit shall comply with such rules, regulations, orders, and instructions of the Equal Employment Opportunity Commission which shall include a provision that an employee or applicant for employment shall be notified of any final action taken on any complaint of discrimination filed by him thereunder. Reasonable exemptions to the provisions of this section may be established by the Commission but only when the Commission has established a maximum age requirement on the basis of a determination that age is a bona fide occupational qualification necessary to the performance of the duties of the position. With respect to employment in the Library of Congress, authorities granted in this subsection to the Equal Employment Opportunity Commission shall be exercised by the Librarian of Congress.

(c) Any person aggrieved may bring a civil action in any Federal district court of competent jurisdiction for such legal or equitable relief as will effectuate the purposes of this chapter.

(d) When the individual has not filed a complaint concerning age discrimination with the Commission, no civil action may be commenced by any individual under this section until the individual has given the Commission not less than thirty days' notice of an intent to file such action. Such notice shall be filed within one hundred and eighty days after the alleged unlawful practice occurred. Upon receiving a notice of intent to sue, the Commission shall promptly notify all persons named therein as prospective defendants in the action and take any appropriate action to assure the elimination of any unlawful practice.

(e) Nothing contained in this section shall relieve any Government agency or official of the responsibility to assure nondiscrimination on account of age in employment as required under any provision of Federal law.

(f) Any personnel action of any department, agency, or other entity referred to in subsection (a) of this section shall not be subject to, or affected by, any provision of this chapter, other than the provisions of section 631(b) of this title [section 12(b)] and the provisions of this section.

(g) (1) The Equal Employment Opportunity Commission shall undertake a study relating to the effects of the amendments made to this section by the Age Discrimination in Employment Act Amendments of 1978, and the effects of section 631(b) of this title [section 12(b)], as added by the Age Discrimination in Employment Act Amendments of 1978.

(2) The Equal Employment Opportunity Commission shall transmit a report to the President and to the Congress containing the findings of the Commission resulting from the study of the Commission under paragraph (1) of this subsection. Such report shall be transmitted no later than January 1, 1980.

APPENDIX 6: SELECTED PROVISIONS - THE AMERICANS WITH DISABILITIES ACT (ADA) OF 1990

SUBCHAPTER 1 - EMPLOYMENT [TITLE I]

SECTION 12111. DEFINITIONS [SECTION 101]

As used in this title:

(1) Commission. The term Commission means the Equal Employment Opportunity Commission established by section 2000e-4 of this title.

(2) Covered entity. The term covered entity means an employer, employment agency, labor organization, or joint labor-management committee.

(3) Direct threat. The term direct threat means a significant risk to the health or safety of others that cannot be eliminated by reasonable accommodation.

(4) Employee. The term employee means an individual employed by an employer. With respect to employment in a foreign country, such term includes an individual who is a citizen of the United States.

(5) Employer.

(A) In general. The term employer means a person engaged in an industry affecting commerce who has 15 or more employees for each working day in each of 20 or more calendar weeks in the current or preceding calendar year, and any agent of such person, except that, for two years following the effective date of this title, an employer means a person engaged in an industry affecting commerce who has 25 or more employees for each working day in each of 20 or more calendar weeks in the current or preceding year, and any agent of such person.

(B) Exceptions. The term employer does not include

(i) the United States, a corporation wholly owned by the government of the United States, or an Indian tribe; or

(ii) a bona fide private membership club (other than a labor organization) that is exempt from taxation under section 501(c) of the Internal Revenue Code of 1986.

(6) Illegal use of drugs.

(A) In general. The term illegal use of drugs means the use of drugs, the possession or distribution of which is unlawful under the Controlled Substances Act (21 U.S.C. 812). Such term does not include the use of a drug taken under supervision by a licensed health care professional, or other uses authorized by the Controlled Substances Act or other provisions of Federal law.

(B) Drugs. The term drug means a controlled substance, as defined in schedules I through V of section 202 of the Controlled Substances Act.

(7) Person, etc. The terms person, labor organization, employment agency, commerce, and industry affecting commerce, shall have the same meaning given such terms in section 701 of the Civil Rights Act of 1964 (42 U.S.C. 2000e).

(8) Qualified individual with a disability. The term qualified individual with a disability means an individual with a disability who, with or without reasonable accommodation, can perform the essential functions of the employment position that such individual holds or desires. For the purposes of this title, consideration shall be given to the employers judgment as to what functions of a job are essential, and if an employer has prepared a written description before advertising or interviewing applicants for the job, this description shall be considered evidence of the essential functions of the job.

(9) Reasonable accommodation. The term reasonable accommodation may include

(A) making existing facilities used by employees readily accessible to and usable by individuals with disabilities; and

(B) job restructuring, part-time or modified work schedules, reassignment to a vacant position, acquisition or modification of equipment or devices, appropriate adjustment or modifications of examinations, training materials or policies, the provision of qualified readers or interpreters, and other similar accommodations for individuals with disabilities.

(10) Undue hardship.

(A) In general. The term undue hardship means an action requiring significant difficulty or expense, when considered in light of the factors set forth in subparagraph (B).

(B) Factors to be considered. In determining whether an accommodation would impose an undue hardship on a covered entity, factors to be considered include

(i) the nature and cost of the accommodation needed under this Act;

(ii) the overall financial resources of the facility or facilities involved in the provision of the reasonable accommodation; the number of persons employed at such facility; the effect on expenses and resources, or the impact otherwise of such accommodation upon the operation of the facility;

(iii) the overall financial resources of the covered entity; the overall size of the business of a covered entity with respect to the number of its employees; the number, type, and location of its facilities; and

(iv) the type of operation or operations of the covered entity, including the composition, structure, and functions of the workforce of such entity; the geographic separateness, administrative, or fiscal relationship of the facility or facilities in question to the covered entity.

SECTION 12112. DISCRIMINATION [SECTION 102]

(a) General Rule. No covered entity shall discriminate against a qualified individual with a disability because of the disability of such individual in regard to job application procedures, the hiring, advancement, or discharge of employees, employee compensation, job training, and other terms, conditions, and privileges of employment.

(b) Construction. As used in subsection (a), the term discriminate includes

(1) limiting, segregating, or classifying a job applicant or employee in a way that adversely affects the opportunities or status of such applicant or employee because of the disability of such applicant or employee;

(2) participating in a contractual or other arrangement or relationship that has the effect of subjecting a covered entity's qualified applicant or employee with a disability to the discrimination prohibited by this title (such relationship includes a relationship with an employment or referral agency, labor union, an organization providing fringe benefits to an employee of the covered entity, or an organization providing training and apprenticeship programs);

(3) utilizing standards, criteria, or methods of administration

(A) that have the effect of discrimination on the basis of disability;

or

(B) that perpetuate the discrimination of others who are subject to common administrative control;

(4) excluding or otherwise denying equal jobs or benefits to a qualified individual because of the known disability of an individual with whom the qualified individual is known to have a relationship or association;

(5) (A) not making reasonable accommodations to the known physical or mental limitations of an otherwise qualified individual with a disability who is an applicant or employee, unless such covered entity can demonstrate that the accommodation would impose an undue hardship on the operation of the business of such covered entity; or

(B) denying employment opportunities to a job applicant or employee who is an otherwise qualified individual with a disability, if such denial is based on the need of such covered entity to make reasonable accommodation to the physical or mental impairments of the employee or applicant;

(6) using qualification standards, employment tests or other selection criteria that screen out or tend to screen out an individual with a disability or a class of individuals with disabilities unless the standard, test or other selection criteria, as used by the covered entity, is shown to be job-related for the position in question and is consistent with business necessity; and

(7) failing to select and administer tests concerning employment in the most effective manner to ensure that, when such test is administered to a job applicant or employee who has a disability that impairs sensory, manual, or speaking skills, such test results accurately reflect the skills, aptitude, or whatever other factor of such applicant or employee that such test purports to measure, rather than reflecting the impaired sensory, manual, or speaking skills of such employee

or applicant (except where such skills are the factors that the test purports to measure).

(c) Covered Entities in Foreign Countries.

(1) In general. It shall not be unlawful under this section for a covered entity to take any action that constitutes discrimination under this section with respect to an employee in a workplace in a foreign country if compliance with this section would cause such covered entity to violate the law of the foreign country in which such workplace is located.

(2) Control of Corporation.

(A) Presumption. If an employer controls a corporation whose place of incorporation is a foreign country, any practice that constitutes discrimination under this section and is engaged in by such corporation shall be presumed to be engaged in by such employer.

(B) Exception. This section shall not apply with respect to the foreign operations of an employer that is a foreign person not controlled by an American employer.

(C) Determination. For purposes of this paragraph, the determination of whether an employer controls a corporation shall be based on -

(i) the interrelation of operations;

(ii) the common management;

(iii) the centralized control of labor relations; and

(iv) the common ownership or financial control of the employer and the corporation.

(d) Medical Examinations and Inquiries.

(1) In general. The prohibition against discrimination as referred to in subsection (a) shall include medical examinations and inquiries.

(2) Preemployment.

(A) Prohibited examination or inquiry. Except as provided in paragraph (3), a covered entity shall not conduct a medical examination or make inquiries of a job applicant as to whether such applicant is an individual with a disability or as to the nature or severity of such disability.

(B) Acceptable inquiry. A covered entity may make preemployment inquiries into the ability of an applicant to perform job-related functions.

(3) Employment entrance examination. A covered entity may require a medical examination after an offer of employment has been made to a job applicant and prior to the commencement of the employment duties of such applicant, and may condition an offer of employment on the results of such examination, if

(A) all entering employees are subjected to such an examination regardless of disability;

(B) information obtained regarding the medical condition or history of the applicant is collected and maintained on separate forms and in separate medical files and is treated as a confidential medical record, except that

(i) supervisors and managers may be informed regarding necessary restrictions on the work or duties of the employee and necessary accommodations;

(ii) first aid and safety personnel may be informed, when appropriate, if the disability might require emergency treatment; and

(iii) government officials investigating compliance with this Act shall be provided relevant information on request; and

(C) the results of such examination are used only in accordance with this title.

(4) Examination and inquiry.

(A) Prohibited examinations and inquiries. A covered entity shall not require a medical examination and shall not make inquiries of an employee as to whether such employee is an individual with a disability or as to the nature or severity of the disability, unless such examination or inquiry is shown to be job-related and consistent with business necessity.

(B) Acceptable examinations and inquiries. A covered entity may conduct voluntary medical examinations, including voluntary medical histories, which are part of an employee health program available to employees at that work site. A covered entity may make inquiries into the ability of an employee to perform job-related functions.

(C) Requirement. Information obtained under subparagraph (B) regarding the medical condition or history of any employee are subject to the requirements of subparagraphs (B) and (C) of paragraph (3).

SECTION 12113. DEFENSES [SECTION 103]

(a) In General. It may be a defense to a charge of discrimination under this Act that an alleged application of qualification standards, tests, or selection criteria that screen out or tend to screen out or otherwise deny a job or benefit to an individual with a disability has been shown to be job-related and consistent with business necessity, and such performance cannot be accomplished by reasonable accommodation, as required under this title.

(b) Qualification Standards. The term qualification standards may include a requirement that an individual shall not pose a direct threat to the health or safety of other individuals in the workplace.

(c) Religious Entities.

(1) In general. This title shall not prohibit a religious corporation, association, educational institution, or society from giving preference in employment to individuals of a particular religion to perform work connected with the carrying on by such corporation, association, educational institution, or society of its activities.

(2) Religious tenets requirement. Under this title, a religious organization may require that all applicants and employees conform to the religious tenets of such organization.

(d) List of Infectious and Communicable Diseases.

(1) In general. The Secretary of Health and Human Services, not later than 6 months after the date of enactment of this Act, shall

(A) review all infectious and communicable diseases which may be transmitted through handling the food supply;

(B) publish a list of infectious and communicable diseases which are transmitted through handling the food supply;

(C) publish the methods by which such diseases are transmitted; and

(D) widely disseminate such information regarding the list of diseases and their modes of transmissibility to the general public.

Such list shall be updated annually.

(2) Applications. In any case in which an individual has an infectious or communicable disease that is transmitted to others through the handling of food, that is included on the list developed by the Secretary of Health and Human Services under paragraph (1), and which cannot be eliminated by reasonable accommodation, a covered entity may refuse to assign or continue to assign such individual to a job involving food handling.

(3) Construction. Nothing in this Act shall be construed to preempt, modify, or amend any State, county, or local law, ordinance, or regulation applicable to food handling which is designed to protect the public health from individuals who pose a significant risk to the health or safety of others, which cannot be eliminated by reasonable accommodation, pursuant to the list of infectious or communicable diseases and the modes of transmissibility published by the Secretary of Health and Human Services

SECTION 12114. ILLEGAL USE OF DRUGS AND ALCOHOL [SECTION 103]

(a) Qualified Individual With a Disability. For purposes of this title, the term qualified individual with a disability shall not include any employee or applicant who is currently engaging in the illegal use of drugs, when the covered entity acts on the basis of such use.

(b) Rules of Construction. Nothing in subsection (a) shall be construed to exclude as a qualified individual with a disability an individual who

(1) has successfully completed a supervised drug rehabilitation program and is no longer engaging in the illegal use of drugs, or has otherwise been rehabilitated successfully and is no longer engaging in such use;

(2) is participating in a supervised rehabilitation program and is no longer engaging in such use; or

(3) is erroneously regarded as engaging in such use, but is not engaging in such use; except that it shall not be a violation of this Act for a covered entity to adopt or administer reasonable policies or procedures, including but not limited to drug testing, designed to ensure that an individual described in paragraph (1) or (2) is no longer engaging in the illegal use of drugs.

(c) Authority of Covered Entity. A covered entity

(1) may prohibit the illegal use of drugs and the use of alcohol at the workplace by all employees;

(2) may require that employees shall not be under the influence of alcohol or be engaging in the illegal use of drugs at the workplace;

(3) may require that employees behave in conformance with the requirements established under the Drug-Free Workplace Act of 1988 (41 U.S.C. 701 et seq.);

(4) may hold an employee who engages in the illegal use of drugs or who is an alcoholic to the same qualification standards for employment or job performance and behavior that such entity holds other employees, even if any unsatisfactory performance or behavior is related to the drug use or alcoholism of such employee; and

(5) may, with respect to Federal regulations regarding alcohol and the illegal use of drugs, require that

(A) employees comply with the standards established in such regulations of the Department of Defense, if the employees of the covered entity are employed in an industry subject to such regulations, including complying with regulations (if any) that apply to employment in sensitive positions in such an industry, in the case of employees of the covered entity who are employed in such positions (as defined in the regulations of the Department of Defense);

(B) employees comply with the standards established in such regulations of the Nuclear Regulatory Commission, if the employees of the covered entity are employed in an industry subject to such regulations, including complying with regulations (if any) that apply to employment in sensitive positions in such an industry, in the case of employees of the covered entity who are employed in such positions (as defined in the regulations of the Nuclear Regulatory Commission); and

(C) employees comply with the standards established in such regulations of the Department of Transportation, if the employees of the covered entity are employed in a transportation industry subject to such regulations, including complying with such regulations (if any) that apply to employment in sensitive positions in such an industry, in the case of employees of the covered entity who are employed in such positions (as defined in the regulations of the Department of Transportation).

(d) Drug Testing.

(1) In general. For purposes of this title, a test to determine the illegal use of drugs shall not be considered a medical examination.

(2) Construction. Nothing in this title shall be construed to encourage, prohibit, or authorize the conducting of drug testing for the illegal use of drugs by job applicants or employees or making employment decisions based on such test results.

(e) Transportation Employees. Nothing in this title shall be construed to encourage, prohibit, restrict, or authorize the otherwise lawful exercise by entities subject to the jurisdiction of the Department of Transportation of authority to

(1) test employees of such entities in, and applicants for, positions involving safety-sensitive duties for the illegal use of drugs and for on-duty impairment by alcohol; and

(2) remove such persons who test positive for illegal use of drugs and on-duty impairment by alcohol pursuant to paragraph (1) from safety-sensitive duties in implementing subsection (c).

SECTION 12115. POSTING NOTICES [SECTION 105]

Every employer, employment agency, labor organization, or joint labor-management committee covered under this title shall post notices in an accessible format to applicants, employees, and members describing the applicable provisions of this Act, in the manner prescribed by section 711 of the Civil Rights Act of 1964 (42 U.S.C. 2000e-10).

SECTION 12116. REGULATIONS [SECTION 106]

Not later than 1 year after the date of enactment of this Act, the Commission shall issue regulations in an accessible format to carry out this title in accordance with subchapter II of chapter 5 of title 5, United States Code.

SECTION 12117. ENFORCEMENT [SECTION 107]

(a) Powers, Remedies, and Procedures. The powers, remedies, and procedures set forth in sections 705, 706, 707, 709, and 710 of the Civil Rights Act of 1964 (42 U.S.C. 2000e-4, 2000e-5, 2000e-6, 2000e-8, and 2000e-9) shall be the powers, remedies, and procedures this title provides to the Commission, to the Attorney General, or to any person alleging discrimination on the basis of disability in violation of any provision of this Act, or regulations promulgated under section 106, concerning employment.

(b) Coordination. The agencies with enforcement authority for actions which allege employment discrimination under this title and under the Rehabilitation Act of 1973 shall develop procedures to ensure that administrative complaints filed under this title and under the Rehabilitation Act of 1973 are dealt with in a manner that avoids duplication of effort and prevents imposition of inconsistent or conflicting standards for the same requirements under this title and the Rehabilitation Act of 1973. The Commission, the Attorney General, and the Office of Federal Contract Compliance Programs shall establish such coordinating mechanisms (similar to provisions contained in the joint regulations promulgated by the Commission and the Attorney General at part 42 of title 28 and part 1691 of title 29, Code of Federal Regulations, and the Memorandum of Understanding between the Commission and the Office of Federal Contract Compliance Programs dated January 16, 1981 (46 Fed. Reg. 7435, January 23, 1981)) in regulations implementing this title and Rehabilitation Act of 1973 not later than 18 months after the date of enactment of this Act.

APPENDIX 7: NOTICE OF RIGHT TO SUE (ISSUED ON REQUEST)

EEOC Form 161-B (10/96) U. S. EQUAL EMPLOYMENT OPPORTUNITY COMMISSION

NOTICE OF RIGHT TO SUE *(ISSUED ON REQUEST)*

To:

From:
U. S. Equal Employment Opportunity Commission
Tampa Area Office
501 E. Polk Street, Room 1020
Tampa, Florida 33602

[ ] *On behalf of person(s) aggrieved whose identity is CONFIDENTIAL (29 CFR § 1601.7(a))*

Charge No.	EEOC Representative	Telephone No.
		(813) 228-2310

(See also the additional information attached to this form.)

NOTICE TO THE PERSON AGGRIEVED:

Title VII of the Civil Rights Act of 1964 and/or the Americans with Disabilities Act (ADA): This is your Notice of Right to Sue, issued under Title VII and/or the ADA based on the above-numbered charge. It has been issued at your request. Your suit under Title VII or the ADA **must be filed in federal or state court WITHIN 90 DAYS of your receipt of this Notice. Otherwise**, your right to sue based on the above-numbered charge will be lost.

[ ] More than 180 days have passed since the filing of this charge.

[ ] Less than 180 days have passed since the filing of this charge, but I have determined that it is unlikely that the EEOC will be able to complete its administrative processing within 180 days from the filing of the charge.

[ ] The EEOC is terminating its processing of this charge.

[x] The EEOC will continue to process this charge.

Age Discrimination in Employment Act (ADEA): You may sue under the ADEA at any time from 60 days after the charge was filed until 90 days after you receive notice that we have completed action on the charge. In this regard, the **paragraph marked below applies to your case:**

[ ] The EEOC is closing your case. Therefore, your lawsuit under the ADEA **must be filed in federal or state court WITHIN 90 DAYS of your receipt of this Notice.** Otherwise, your right to sue based on the above-numbered charge will be lost.

[ ] The EEOC is continuing its handling of your ADEA case. However, if 60 days have passed since the filing of your charge, you may file suit in federal or state court under the ADEA at this time.

Equal Pay Act (EPA): You already have the right to sue under the EPA (filing an EEOC charge is not required). EPA suits must be brought in federal or state court within 2 years (3 years for willful violations) of the alleged EPA underpayment. This means that **backpay due for any violations that occurred more than 2 years (3 years) before you file suit may not be collectible.**

If you file suit based this charge, please send a copy of your court complaint to this office.

On behalf of the Commission

J. D. Smith

J. D. Smith, Area Director *(Date Mailed)*

Enclosure(s)
Copy of Charge

cc:

APPENDIX 8: DIRECTORY OF EEOC MEDIATION PROGRAM - FIELD AND DISTRICT OFFICES

OFFICE	ADDRESS	TELEPHONE	TTY	FAX
Atlanta District Office	100 Alabama Street SW, Suite 4R30 Atlanta, Georgia 30303	404-562-6814	404-562-6801	404-562-6974
Baltimore Field Office	10 South Howard St., 3rd Floor Baltimore, Maryland 21201	410-962-6066	410-962-6065	410-962-3706
Birmingham District Office	1130 22nd St. South, Suite 2000 Birmingham, Alabama 35205	205-212-2033	205-212-2105	205-212-2025
Charlotte District Office	129 West Trade Street, Suite 400 Charlotte, North Carolina 28202	704-344-6689	704-344-6684	704-344-6750
Chicago District Office	500 West Madison St., Suite 2800 Chicago, Illinois 60661	312-353-7695	312-353-2421	312-353-6676
Cleveland Field Office	1240 E. 9th St., Suite 3001 Cleveland, Ohio 44119	216-522-7678	216-522-8441	216-522-7389

OFFICE	ADDRESS	TELEPHONE	TTY	FAX
Dallas District Office	5410 Fredericksburg Rd., Suite 200 San Antonio, Texas 78229	210-281-2507	210-281-7610	210-281-2512
Denver Field Office	3300 N. Central Ave., Suite 690 Phoenix, Arizona 85012	602-640-5022	602-640-5072	602-640-4729
Detroit Field Office	477 Michigan Ave., Room 865 Detroit, Michigan 48226	313-226-4087	313-226-7599	313-226-3045
Houston District Office	1919 Smith Street, 7th Floor Houston, Texas 77002	713-209-3433	713-209-3439	713-209-3317
Indianapolis District Office	101 West Ohio St., Suite 1900 Indianapolis, Indiana 46204	317-226-6422	317-226-5162	317-226-5471
Los Angeles District Office	255 E. Temple Street, 4th Floor Los Angeles, California 90012	213-894-1030	213-894-1121	213-894-8385
Memphis District Office	1407 Union Ave., Suite 621 Memphis, Tennessee 38104	901-544-0152	901-544-0112	901-544-0126
Miami District Office	2 South Biscayne Blvd., Suite 2700 Miami, Florida 33131	305-530-6002	305-536-5721	305-530-6121
Milwaukee Area Office	310 West Wisconsin Ave., Suite 800 Milwaukee, Wisconsin	414-297-1276	414-297-1115	414-297-3125
New Orleans Field Office	1555 Poydras St., Suite 1900 New Orleans, Louisiana 70112	504-595-2846	504-589-2958	504-589-6861

OFFICE	ADDRESS	TELEPHONE	TTY	FAX
New York District Office	33 Whitehall Street New York, New York 10004	212-336-3645	212-336-3622	212-336-3633
Oklahoma Area Office	1222 Spruce St., Room 8.100 St. Louis, Missouri 63103	314-539-7931	314-539-7803	314-539-7894
Philadelphia District Office	801 Market Street, Suite 1300 Philadelphia, Pennsylvania 19107	215-440-2819	215-440-2610	215-440-2822
Phoenix District Office	3300 N. Central Ave., Suite 690 Phoenix, Arizona 85012	602-640-5022	602-640-5072	602-640-4729
San Francisco District Office	350 The Embarcadero, Suite 500 San Francisco, California 94105	415-625-5660	415-625-5610	415-625-5631
Seattle Field Office	909 First Avenue, Suite 400 Seattle, Washington 98104	206-220-6858	206-220-6882	206-220-6955
St. Louis District Office	1222 Spruce St., Room 8.100 St. Louis, Missouri 63103	314-539-7931	314-539-7803	314-539-7894
Washington Field Office	1801 L Street NW, Suite 100 Washington, DC 20507	202-419-0702	202-419-0702	202-419-0740

Source: U.S. Equal Employment Opportunity Commission.

APPENDIX 9: TABLE OF EEOC MEDIATION STATISTICS (FISCAL YEARS 1999–2003)

DISPOSITION	FY 1999	FY 2000	FY 2001	FY 2002	FY 2003
Total Resolutions	4833	7438	6987	7858	7990
Mediations Conducted	7397	11,478	10,588	11,457	11,595
Resolution Rate	65.3%	64.8%	65.9%	68.5%	68.9%
Average Closure Rate	86 days	96 days	84 days	82 days	85 days
Monetary Benefits (millions)	$58.6	$108.4	$90.3	$111.5	$115.9
Persons Benefited Monetarily	4271	6175	5897	6967	6896
Persons Benefited Non-Monetarily	993	1034	927	1002	1005

Source: U.S. Equal Employment Opportunity Commission

APPENDIX 10: UNIVERSAL AGREEMENT TO MEDIATE

The United States Equal Employment Opportunity Commission and [name of employer] enter into this Universal Agreement to Mediate. This Universal Agreement to Mediate applies to charges of discrimination filed with the EEOC, or any charge of discrimination filed with a Fair Employment Practice Agency and then deferred to the EEOC for processing that the EEOC deems eligible for the mediation program.

As the EEOC Alternative Dispute Resolution (ADR) Mediation Program provides a method for employer and charging party to come together and informally resolve their workplace disputes, and as (name of employer) has an interest in resolving workplace disputes that may arise in a fair and efficient manner, the EEOC and [name of employer] agree as follows:

1 All eligible charges of discrimination filed with the EEOC in which [name of employer] is named as an employer/respondent will be referred to the EEOC' Mediation Program. This Universal Agreement to Mediate will operate as a general agreement and is used in lieu of an individual Agreement to Mediate for all charges of discrimination filed against [name of employer].

2 The EEOC mediation program is a voluntary program. Therefore, [name of employer] and the charging party have the right to refuse to mediate any charge of discrimination. If either party rejects mediation, the charge is ineligible to enter the EEOC mediation program and will be forwarded to an enforcement unit for investigation.

3 Charges of discrimination filed against [name of employer] that would normally be dismissed under the Commission's Priority Charge Handling Procedures will not be eligible to enter the EEOC mediation program.

4 All inquiries and scheduling of mediations shall be scheduled through [name & title], designated representative(s) for [name of employer], as soon as practical after the charge is filed and the charging party has agreed to participate, but in any event no later than 45 days from the date the charge enters the mediation program. The phone and fax numbers and email for [name of representative] are [insert numbers and email address].

5 All inquiries regarding the EEOC Mediation Program shall be directed to the ADR Coordinator in the EEOC District Office where the charge was filed.

District Director	Representative for [Company Name]
Date:	Date:

Source: U.S. Equal Employment Opportunity Commission

APPENDIX 11: LIST OF SIGNATORIES TO THE EEOC NATIONAL UNIVERSAL AGREEMENT TO MEDIATE

The following companies have embraced the EEOC Mediation Program by signing a non-confidential National Universal Agreement to Mediate (NUAM):

99 Restaurant & Pub

Administaff

Albertsons, Inc. (includes Jewel Food Stores, OSCO Drug Stores, Acme Markets, Jewel-Osco, Sav-on Drug Stores, and Super Saver Foods)

Alliance Residential Management

Alpha International Travel

Banta Corporation

Black & Veatch Corporation

Books-A-Million, Inc.

Cardinal Freight Carriers, Inc.

CenterPoint Energy

ConAgra Foods, Inc.

CRST International, Inc.

Deluxe Media Services, Inc.

Education America/Remington College

Ford Motor Company

Frito-Lay, Inc.

Global Mortgage Group

Golden Corral Corporation

Halliburton

Heartland Food Corporation

Huddle House, Inc.

Intel Corporation

Inteli Risk Management

International Dairy Queen (includes Orange Julius, Karmelkorn Shoppes, and Golden Skillet)

Kimble Glass, Inc.

Labor Ready, Inc.

Lending Tree, Inc.

Lucor, Inc. d/b/a Jiffy Lube

McDonald's USA (Regional Agreement)

New Penn Motor Express, Inc.

Northwestern Mutual Life Insurance Company

O'Charlely's, Inc.

Pitney Bowes, Inc.

Quest Diagnostics, Inc.

Rent-Way, Inc.

Roadway Express, Inc.

Ryan's Restaurant Group, Inc.

ScanSource

Sentry Insurance

Southern Company

Starkey Laboratories

State of California, Public Utilities Commission

Steak 'n Shake

Toyota Financial Services

Trim Masters, Inc.

Tyson Foods, Inc.

United Services Automobile Association

W.S. Badcock Corporation

Wheaton Franciscan Healthcare

Source: U.S. Equal Employment Opportunity Commission

APPENDIX 12: TABLE OF RACE-BASED DISCRIMINATION CHARGES AND RESOLUTIONS (2000–2006)

The following chart represents the total number of charge receipts filed and resolved under Title VII alleging race-based discrimination.

DISPOSITION	2000	2001	2002	2003	2004	2005	2006
Total Charges Received	28,945	28,912	29,910	28,526	27,696	26,740	27,238
Total Resolutions	33,188	32,077	33,199	30,702	29,631	27,411	25,992
Settlements	2802 (8.4%)	2549 (7.9%)	3059 (9.2%)	2890 (9.4%)	2927 (9.9%)	2801 (10.2%)	3039 (11.7%)
Withdrawals With Benefits	1150 (3.5%)	1203 (3.8%)	1200 (3.6%)	1125 (3.7%)	1088 (3.7%)	1167 (4.3%)	1177 (4.5%)
Administrative Closures	5727 (17.3%)	5626 (17.5%)	5043 (15.2%)	4759 (15.5%)	4261 (14.4%)	3674 (13.4%)	3436 (13.2%)
No Reasonable Cause	21,319 (64.2%)	20,302 (63.3%)	21,853 (65.8%)	20,506 (66.8%)	20,166 (68.1%)	18,608 (67.9%)	17,324 (66.7%)
Reasonable Cause	2190 (6.6%)	2397 (7.5%)	2044 (6.2%)	1422 (4.6%)	1189 (4.0%)	1161 (4.2%)	1016 (3.9%)
Successful Conciliations	529 (1.6%)	691 (2.2%)	580 (1.7%)	392 (1.3%)	330 (1.1%)	377 (1.4%)	292 (1.1%)

DISPOSITION	2000	2001	2002	2003	2004	2005	2006
Unsuccessful Conciliations	1661 (5.0%)	1706 (5.3%)	1464 (4.4%)	1030 (3.4%)	859 (2.9%)	784 (2.9%)	724 (2.8%)
Merit Resolutions	6142 (18.5%)	6149 (19.2%)	6303 (19.0%)	5437 (17.7%)	5204 (17.6%)	5129 (18.7%)	5232 (20.1%)
Monetary Benefit (Millions)*	$61.7	$86.5	$81.1	$69.6	$61.1	$76.5	$61.4

* Figure does not include monetary benefits obtained through litigation.

Source: U.S. Equal Employment Opportunity Commission Office

APPENDIX 13: TABLE OF RELIGION-BASED DISCRIMINATION CHARGES AND RESOLUTIONS (2000–2006)

The following chart represents the total number of charge receipts filed and resolved under Title VII alleging religion-based discrimination.

DISPOSITION	2000	2001	2002	2003	2004	2005	2006
Total Charges Received	1939	2127	2572	2532	2466	2340	2541
Total Resolutions	2230	2217	2729	2690	2676	2352	2387
Settlements	156 (7.0%)	182 (8.2%)	237 (8.7%)	221 (8.2%)	241 (9.0%)	227 (9.7%)	244 (10.2%)
Withdrawals with Benefits	94 (4.2%)	77 (3.5%)	100 (3.7%)	86 (3.2%)	101 (3.8%)	98 (4.2%)	118 (4.9%)
Administrative Closures	429 (19.2%)	382 (17.2%)	451 (16.5%)	434 (16.1%)	490 (18.3%)	384 (16.3%)	364 (15.2%)
No Reasonable Cause	1343 (60.2%)	1349 (60.8%)	1729 (63.4%)	1744 (64.8%)	1672 (62.5%)	1442 (61.3%)	1524 (63.8%)
Reasonable Cause	208 (9.3%)	227 (10.2%)	212 (7.8%)	205 (7.6%)	172 (6.4%)	201 (8.5%)	137 (5.7%)
Successful Conciliations	56 (2.5%)	43 (1.9%)	54 (2.0%)	67 (2.5%)	38 (1.4%)	36 (1.5%)	38 (1.6%)
Unsuccessful Conciliations	152 (6.8%)	184 (8.3%)	158 (5.8%)	138 (5.1%)	134 (5.0%)	165 (7.0%)	99 (4.1%)

DISPOSITION	2000	2001	2002	2003	2004	2005	2006
Merit Resolutions	458 (20.5%)	486 (21.9%)	549 (20.1%)	512 (19.0%)	514 (19.2%)	526 (22.4%)	499 (20.9%)
Monetary Benefit (Millions)*	$5.5	$14.1	$4.3	$6.6	$6.0	$6.1	$5.7

* Figure does not include monetary benefits obtained through litigation.

Source: U.S. Equal Employment Opportunity Commission

APPENDIX 14: TABLE OF SEX-BASED DISCRIMINATION CHARGES AND RESOLUTIONS (2000–2006)

The following chart represents the total number of charge receipts filed and resolved under Title VII alleging sex-based discrimination.

DISPOSITION	2000	2001	2002	2003	2004	2005	2006
Total Charges Received	25,194	25,140	25,536	24,362	24,249	23,094	23,247
Total Resolutions	29,631	28,602	29,088	27,146	26,598	23,743	23,364
Settlements	2644 (8.9%)	2404 (8.4%)	2720 (9.4%)	2877 (10.6%)	3008 (11.3%)	2601 (11.0%)	2828 (12.1%)
Withdrawals with Benefits	1332 (4.5%)	1321 (4.6%)	1304 (4.5%)	1329 (4.9%)	1347 (5.1%)	1418 (6.0%)	1460 (6.2%)
Administrative Closures	6897 (23.3%)	6391 (22.3%)	5819 (20.0%)	5484 (20.2%)	5052 (19.0%)	4188 (17.6%)	4409 (18.9%)
No Reasonable Cause	15,980 (53.9%)	15,654 (54.7%)	16,752 (57.6%)	15,506 (57.1%)	15,481 (58.2%)	13,853 (58.3%)	13,191 (56.5%)
Reasonable Cause	2778 (9.4%)	2832 (9.9%)	2493 (8.6%)	1950 (7.2%)	1710 (6.4%)	1683 (7.1%)	1476 (6.3%)
Successful Conciliations	707 (2.4%)	739 (2.6%)	686 (2.4%)	520 (1.9%)	491 (1.8%)	454 (1.9%)	437 (1.9%)
Unsuccessful Conciliations	2071 (7.0%)	2093 (7.3%)	1807 (6.2%)	1430 (5.3%)	1219 (4.6%)	1229 (5.2%)	1039 (4.4%)

DISPOSITION	2000	2001	2002	2003	2004	2005	2006
Merit Resolutions	6754 (22.8%)	6557 (22.9%)	6517 (22.4%)	6156 (22.7%)	6065 (22.8%)	5702 (24.0%)	5764 (24.7%)
Monetary Benefit (Millions)*	$109.0	$94.4	$94.7	$98.4	$100.8	$91.3	$99.1

* Figure does not include monetary benefits obtained through litigation.

Source: U.S. Equal Employment Opportunity Commission

APPENDIX 15: TABLE OF SEXUAL HARASSMENT CHARGES AND RESOLUTIONS (2000–2006)

The following chart represents the total number of charge receipts filed and resolved under Title VII alleging sexual harassment discrimination as an issue. The data in the sexual harassment table reflect charges filed with EEOC and the state and local Fair Employment Practices agencies around the country that have a work sharing agreement with the Commission.

DISPOSITION	2000	2001	2002	2003	2004	2005	2006
Total Charges Received	15,836	15,475	14,396	13,566	13,136	12,679	12,025
% Charges Filed by Males	13.6%	13.7%	14.9%	14.7%	15.1%	14.3%	15.4%
Total Resolutions	16,726	16,383	15,792	14,534	13,786	12,859	11,936
Settlements	1676 (10.0%)	1568 (9.6%)	1692 (10.7%)	1783 (12.3%)	1646 (11.9%)	1471 (11.4%)	1458 (12.2%)
Withdrawals with Benefits	1389 (8.3%)	1454 (8.9%)	1235 (7.8%)	1300 (8.9%)	1138 (8.3%)	1146 (8.9%)	1175 (9.8%)
Administrative Closures	4632 (27.7%)	4306 (26.3%)	3957 (25.1%)	3600 (24.8%)	33256 (23.6%)	2808 (21.8%)	2838 (23.8%)
No Reasonable Cause	7370 (44.1%)	7309 (44.6%)	7445 (47.1%)	6703 (46.1%)	6708 (48.7%)	6364 (49.5%)	5668 (47.5%)

DISPOSITION	2000	2001	2002	2003	2004	2005	2006
Reasonable Cause	1659 (9.9%)	1746 (10.7%)	1463 (9.3%)	1148 (7.9%)	1037 (7.5%)	1070 (8.3%)	797 (6.7%)
Successful Conciliations	524 (3.1%)	551 (3.4%)	455 (2.9%)	350 (2.4%)	311 (2.3%)	324 (2.5%)	253 (2.1%)
Unsuccessful Conciliations	1135 (6.8%)	1195 (7.3%)	1008 (6.4%)	798 (5.5%)	726 (5.3%)	746 (5.8%)	544 (4.6%)
Merit Resolutions	4724 (28.2%)	4768 (29.1%)	4390 (27.8%)	4231 (29.1%)	3821 (27.7%)	3687 (28.7%)	3430 (28.7%)
Monetary Benefits (Millions)*	$54.6	$53.0	$50.3	$50.0	$37.1	$47.9	$48.8

* Figure does not include monetary benefits obtained through litigation.

Source: U.S. Equal Employment Opportunity Commission

APPENDIX 16: TABLE OF PREGNANCY-BASED DISCRIMINATION CHARGES AND RESOLUTIONS (2000–2006)

The following chart represents the total number of charge receipts filed and resolved under Title VII alleging pregnancy discrimination as an issue. The data in the pregnancy discrimination table reflect charges filed with EEOC and the state and local Fair Employment Practices Agencies around the country that have a work sharing agreement with the commission.

DISPOSITION	2000	2001	2002	2003	2004	2005	2006
Total Charges Received	4160	4287	4714	4649	4887	4730	4901
Total Resolutions	4480	4280	4778	4847	4877	4625	4629
Settlements	602 (13.4%)	518 (12.1%)	607 (12.7%)	685 (14.1%)	756 (15.5%)	656 (14.2%)	650 (14.0%)
Withdrawals with Benefits	322 (7.2%)	327 (7.6%)	408 (8.5%)	429 (8.9%)	420 (8.6%)	413 (8.9%)	426 (9.2%)
Administrative Closures	824 (18.4%)	764 (17.9%)	846 (17.7%)	901 (18.6%)	787 (16.1%)	765 (16.5%)	790 (17.1%)
No Reasonable Cause	2452 (54.7%)	2373 (55.4%)	2634 (55.1%)	2629 (54.2%)	2723 (55.8%)	2570 (55.6%)	2574 (55.6%)
Reasonable Cause	280 (6.3%)	298 (7.0%)	283 (5.9%)	203 (4.2%)	191 (3.9%)	221 (4.8%)	189 (4.1%)

DISPOSITION	2000	2001	2002	2003	2004	2005	2006
Successful Conciliations	110 (2.5%)	123 (2.9%)	126 (2.6%)	75 (1.5%)	87 (1.8%)	92 (2.0%)	74 (1.6%)
Unsuccessful Conciliations	170 (3.8%)	175 (4.1%)	157 (3.3%)	128 (2.6%)	104 (2.1%)	129 (2.8%)	115 (2.5%)
Merit Resolutions	1204 (26.9%)	1143 (26.7%)	1298 (27.2%)	1317 (27.2%)	1367 (28.0%)	1290 (27.9%)	1265 (27.3%)
Monetary Benefits (Millions)*	$20.6	$7.5	$10.0	$12.4	$11.7	$11.8	$10.4

* Figure does not include monetary benefits obtained through litigation.

Source: U.S. Equal Employment Opportunity Commission

APPENDIX 17: TABLE OF EQUAL PAY ACT CHARGES AND RESOLUTIONS (2000–2006)

The following chart represents the total number of charge receipts filed and resolved under the EPA. Receipts include all charges filed under the EPA and those filed concurrently under Title VII, ADA, and ADEA. Therefore, the sum of receipts for all statutes will exceed total charges received.

DISPOSITION	2000	2001	2002	2003	2004	2005	2006
Total Charges Received	1270	1251	1256	1167	1011	970	861
Total Resolutions	1235	1158	1182	1071	996	889	748
Settlements	80 (6.5%)	96 (8.3%)	117 (9.9%)	124 (11.6%)	109 (10.9%)	101 (11.4%)	88 (11.8%)
Withdrawals with Benefits	70 (5.7%)	62 (5.4%)	73 (6.2%)	44 (4.1%)	65 (6.5%)	44 (4.9%)	38 (5.1%)
Administrative Closures	250 (20.2%)	201 (17.4%)	210 (17.8%)	178 (16.6%)	166 (16.7%)	147 (16.5%)	113 (15.1%)
No Reasonable Cause	716 (58.0%)	679 (58.6%)	682 (57.7%)	613 (57.2%)	573 (57.5%)	521 (58.6%)	463 (61.9%)
Reasonable Cause	119 (9.6%)	120 (10.4%)	100 (8.5%)	112 (10.5%)	83 (8.3%)	76 (8.5%)	47 (6.3%)
Successful Conciliations	45 (3.6%)	37 (3.2%)	23 (1.9%)	29 (2.7%)	24 (2.4%)	23 (2.6%)	16 (2.1%)

DISPOSITION	2000	2001	2002	2003	2004	2005	2006
Unsuccessful Conciliations	74 (6.0%)	83 (7.2%)	77 (6.5%)	83 (7.7%)	59 (5.9%)	53 (6.0%)	31 (4.1%)
Merit Resolutions	269 (21.8%)	278 (24.0%)	290 (24.5%)	280 (26.1%)	257 (25.8%)	221 (24.9%)	173 (23.1%)
Monetary Benefits (Millions)*	$3.6	$5.1	$10.3	$3.4	$6.4	$3.1	$3.1

* Figure does not include monetary benefits obtained through litigation.

Source: U.S. Equal Employment Opportunity Commission

APPENDIX 18: TABLE OF NATIONAL ORIGIN-BASED DISCRIMINATION CHARGES AND RESOLUTIONS (2000–2006)

The following chart represents the total number of charge receipts filed and resolved under Title VII alleging national origin-based discrimination.

DISPOSITION	2000	2001	2002	2003	2004	2005	2006
Total Charges Received	7792	8025	9046	8450	8361	8035	8327
Total Resolutions	8691	8899	9952	9172	8943	8319	8181
Settlements	630 (7.2%)	668 (7.5%)	817 (8.2%)	839 (9.1%)	815 (9.1%)	803 (9.7%)	778 (9.5%)
Withdrawals with Benefits	276 (3.2%)	341 (3.8%)	350 (3.5%)	333 (3.6%)	362 (4.0%)	423 (5.1%)	376 (4.6%)
Administrative Closures	1538 (17.7%)	1448 (16.3%)	1561 (15.7%)	1353 (14.8%)	1365 (15.3%)	1240 (14.9%)	1157 (14.1%)
No Reasonable Cause	5502 (63.3%)	5461 (61.4%)	6290 (63.2%)	6117 (66.7%)	5951 (66.5%)	5316 (63.9%)	5358 (65.5%)
Reasonable Cause	745 (8.6%)	981 (11.0%)	934 (9.4%)	530 (5.8%)	450 (5.0%)	(537 (6.5%)	512 (6.3%)
Successful Conciliations	159 (1.8%)	229 (2.6%)	168 (1.7%)	112 (1.2%)	145 (1.6%)	122 (1.5%)	106 (1.3%)
Unsuccessful Conciliations	586 (6.7%)	752 (8.5%)	766 (7.7%)	418 (4.6%)	305 (3.4%)	415 (5.0%)	406 (5.0%)

DISPOSITION	2000	2001	2002	2003	2004	2005	2006
Merit Resolutions	1651 (19.0%)	1990 (22.4%)	2101 (21.1%)	1702 (18.6%)	1627 (18.2%)	1763 (21.2%)	1666 (20.4%)
Monetary Benefits (Millions)*	$15.7	$48.1	$21.0	$21.3	$22.3	$19.4	$21.2

* Figure does not include monetary benefits obtained through litigation.

Source: U.S. Equal Employment Opportunity Commission

APPENDIX 19: TABLE OF AGE DISCRIMINATION IN EMPLOYMENT ACT (ADEA) CHARGES AND RESOLUTIONS (2000–2006)

The following chart represents the total number of charge receipts filed and resolved under The Age Discrimination in Employment Act (ADEA) alleging age-based discrimination.

DISPOSITION	2000	2001	2002	2003	2004	2005	2006
Total Charges Received	16,008	17,405	19.921	19.124	17,837	16,585	16,548
Total Resolutions	14,672	15,155	18,673	17,352	15,792	14,076	14,146
Settlements	1156 (7.9%)	1006 (6.6%)	1222 (6.5%)	1285 (7.4%)	1377 (8.7%)	1326 (9.4%)	1417 (10.0%)
Withdrawals with Benefits	560 (3.8%)	551 (3.6%)	671 (3.6%)	710 (4.1%)	787 (5.0%)	764 (5.4%)	767 (5.4%)
Administrative Closures	3232 (22.0%)	3963 (26.1%)	6254 (33.5%)	2824 (16.3%)	3550 (22.5%)	2537 (18.0%)	2639 (18.7%)
No Reasonable Cause	8517 (58.0%)	8388 (55.3%)	9725 (52.1%)	11,976 (69.0%)	9563 (60.6%)	8866 (63.0%)	8746 (61.8%)
Reasonable Cause	1207 (8.2%)	1247 (8.2%)	801 (4.3%)	557 (3.2%)	515 (3.3%)	583 (4.1%)	612 (4.3%)
Successful Conciliations	241 (1.6%)	409 (2.7%)	208 (1.1%)	166 (1.0%)	139 (0.9%)	169 (1.2%)	177 (1.3%)
Unsuccessful Conciliations	966 (6.6%)	838 (5.5%)	593 (3.2%)	391 (2.3%)	376 (2.4%)	414 (2.9%)	435 (3.1%)

DISPOSITION	2000	2001	2002	2003	2004	2005	2006
Merit Resolutions	2923 (19.9%)	2804 (18.5%)	2694 (14.4%)	2552 (14.7%)	2679 (17.0%)	2673 (19.0%)	1796 (19.8%)
Monetary Benefits (Millions)*	$45.2	$53.7	$55.7	$48.9	$69.0	$77.7	$51.5

* Figure does not include monetary benefits obtained through litigation.

Source: U.S. Equal Employment Opportunity Commission

APPENDIX 20: TABLE OF AMERICANS WITH DISABILITIES ACT (ADA) DISCRIMINATION CHARGES AND RESOLUTIONS (2000–2006)

The following chart represents the total number of charge receipts filed and resolved under The Americans with Disabilites Act (ADA) alleging disability-based discrimination.

DISPOSITION	2000	2001	2002	2003	2004	2005	2006
Total Charges Received	15,864	16,470	15,964	15,377	15,376	14,893	15,575
Total Resolutions	20,475	19,084	18,804	16,915	16,949	15,357	15,045
Settlements	1852 (9.0%)	1722 (9.0%)	1705 (9.1%)	1748 (10.3%)	1800 (10.6%)	1685 (11.0%)	1812 (12.0%)
Withdrawals with Benefits	862 (4.2%)	834 (4.4%)	833 (4.4%)	750 (4.4%)	814 (4.8%)	846 (5.5%)	866 (5.8%)
Administrative Closures	4209 (20.6%)	3662 (19.2%)	3335 (17.7%)	2995 (17.7%)	3083 (18.2%)	2691 (17.5%)	2452 (16.3%)
No Reasonable Cause	11,431 (55.8%)	10,332 (54.1%)	11,346 (60.3%)	10,251 (60.6%)	10,318 (60.9%)	9,268 (60.4%)	9,077 (60.3%)
Reasonable Cause	2121 (10.4%)	2534 (13.3%)	1585 (8.4%)	1171 (6.9%)	934 (5.5%)	867 (5.6%)	850 (5.6%)
Successful Conciliations	663 (3.2%)	741 (3.9%)	644 (3.4%)	487 (2.9%)	357 (2.1%)	338 (2.2%)	330 (2.2%)

DISPOSITION	2000	2001	2002	2003	2004	2005	2006
Unsuccessful Conciliations	1458 (7.1%)	1793 (9.4%)	941 (5.0%)	684 (4.0%)	577 (3.4%)	529 (3.4%)	520 (3.5%)
Merit Resolutions	4835 (23.6%)	5090 (26.7%)	4123 (21.9%)	3669 (21.7%)	3548 (20.9%)	3398 (22.1%)	3528 (23.4%)
Monetary Benefits (Millions)*	$41.3	$47.9	$50.0	$45.3	$47.7	$44.8	$48.8

* Figure does not include monetary benefits obtained through litigation.

Source: U.S. Equal Employment Opportunity Commission

GLOSSARY

Action at Law—A judicial proceeding whereby one party prosecutes another for a wrong done.

Actionable—Giving rise to a cause of action.

Administrative Closure—Refers to a charge that is closed for administrative reasons, which may include: the failure to locate the charging party; the charging party failed to respond to EEOC communications; the charging party refused to accept full relief; the charging party requests withdrawal of a charge without receiving benefits or having resolved the issue; there is no statutory jurisdiction. In addition, a charge may be closed due to the outcome of related litigation that establishes a precedent that makes further processing of the charge futile.

Age Discrimination in Employment Act (ADEA)—A federal law that provides that workers over the age of 40 cannot be arbitrarily discriminated against because of age in connection with any employment decision.

American Arbitration Association (AAA)—National organization of arbitrators from whose panel arbitrators are selected for labor and civil disputes.

American Civil Liberties Union (ACLU)—A nationwide organization dedicated to the enforcement and preservation of rights and civil liberties guaranteed by the federal and state constitutions.

Americans with Disabilities Act (ADA)—A federal law that prohibits employers from discriminating on the basis of a "qualified" disability as set forth in the statute.

Appeal—Resort to a higher court for the purpose of obtaining a review of a lower court decision.

Appellate Court—A court having jurisdiction to review the law as applied to a prior determination of the same case.

Arbitration—The reference of a dispute to an impartial person chosen by the parties to the dispute who agree in advance to abide by the arbitrator's award issued after a hearing at which both parties have an opportunity to be heard.

Background Check—Verification of the accuracy of the information a job applicant provides a prospective employer on his or her employment application.

Back Pay—Wages awarded to an employee who was illegally discharged.

Base Rate Pay—An employee's basic hourly rate excluding overtime.

Benefits—An integral part of an employee's compensation package which may include paid vacations, paid holidays, paid personal days, paid sick leave, life insurance, medical and dental insurance coverage, retirement and pension plans, tuition assistance, stock options, etc.

Blue-Collar Workers—Generally refers to individuals engaged in manual labor.

Breach of Duty—In a general sense, any violation or omission of a legal or moral duty.

Bumping Rights—Bumping rights, often created through a seniority system, provide for one employee to displace another employee due to a layoff or other employment action.

Bureau of Labor Statistics—A division of the U.S. Department of Labor that compiles statistics related to employment.

Charge—Under Title VII, refers to a formal allegation filed with the EEOC by a charging party claiming to have been discriminated against by an employer, labor union or employment agency when applying for a job or on the job because of race, color, religion, sex, or national origin.

Civil Rights Act of 1964—The federal act passed to provide stronger protection for rights guaranteed by the Constitution.

Collective Bargaining—In labor law, refers to the negotiation between employers and employees conducted by a union representative designated by a majority of the employees.

Collective Bargaining Agreement—An Agreement between an employer and a labor union which regulates terms and conditions of employment.

Compensation Package—The combination of salary and benefits an employee receives from an employer.

Constitution—The fundamental principles of law that frame a governmental system.

Constitutional Right—Refers to the individual liberties granted by the constitution of a state or the federal government.

Constructive Discharge—In general, a constructive discharge occurs when a worker's resignation or retirement is found to be involuntary because the employer has created a hostile or intolerable work environment or has applied other forms of pressure or coercion that forced the employee to quit or resign.

Court—The branch of government responsible for the resolution of disputes arising under the laws of the government.

Defamation—A libelous (written) or slanderous (spoken) statement that maligns the character of another.

Disability—A medical impairment or disability that results in an individual's inability to carry on their usual activities, requires medical treatment, or adversely affects the individual's ability to earn a living.

Employability—The ability of an employee to meet the demands of a job and the conditions of employment.

Employee—Any individual employed by an employer.

Employment Benefits—All benefits provided or made available to employees by an employer, including group life insurance, health insurance, disability insurance, sick leave, annual leave, educational benefits, and pensions, regardless of whether such benefits are provided by a practice or written policy of an employer or through an employee benefit plan.

Employment Discrimination—Under Title VII, employment discrimination occurs when an employer denies an individual employment opportunities or otherwise affects their terms and conditions of employment based on race, color, religion, sex, or national origin.

Equal Employment Opportunity Commission (EEOC)—Federal agency responsible for interpreting and enforcing the employment anti-discrimination provisions under federal law, including Title VII of the Civil Rights Act of 1964.

Fair Labor Standards Act (FLSA)—Federal law governing federal wage and hour regulations.

FEPA—A state or local fair employment practices agency where may charges are first deferred for a specific time period for handling prior to being forwarded to the EEOC.

FMLA—The Family and Medical Leave Act of 1993, Public Law 103-3 (February 5, 1993), 107 Stat. 6 (29 U.S.C. 2601 et seq.).

Hostile Work Environment—A working environment that a reasonable person would find both hostile or abusive, and one that the particular person who is the object of the harassment perceives to be hostile or abusive. Hostile work environment is determined by looking at all of the circumstances, including the frequency of the allegedly harassing conduct, its severity, whether it is physically threatening or humiliating, and whether it unreasonably interferes with an employee's work performance. In a sexual harassment claim, a hostile work environment is one in which the victim is subjected to unwelcome and severe or pervasive repeated sexual comments, innuendoes, touching, or other conduct of a sexual nature which creates an intimidating or offensive place for employees to work.

Impairment—The loss, or loss of use of, any body part, system, or function.

Independent Contractor—An individual who contracts to perform services for others without qualifying legally as an employee.

Investigation—Under Title VII, refers to an official inquiry by the EEOC to determine whether a charging party's allegations are supported by the available evidence.

Job Skills—The skills an employee needs to perform a particular job.

Labor Organization—An association of workers for the purpose of bargaining the terms and conditions of employment on behalf of labor and management.

Layoff—A forced furlough from employment, on a temporary basis, generally caused by a lack of available work.

Mediation—The act of a third person in intermediating between two contending parties with a view to persuading them to adjust or settle their dispute but without the authority to make a binding decision.

Mediation/Arbitration—Combination of mediation and arbitration that utilizes a neutral selected to serve as both mediator and arbitrator in a dispute.

Mediator—One who interposes between parties at variance for the purpose of reconciling them.

Merit Resolution—A charge with an outcome favorable to the charging parties and/or a charge with meritorious allegations. A merit resolution may include negotiated settlements, withdrawals with benefits, successful conciliations, and unsuccessful conciliations.

National Labor Relations Act—A federal statute known as the Wagner Act of 1935 and amended by the Taft-Hartley Act of 1947, which established the National Labor Relations Board to regulate the relations between employers and employees.

National Labor Relations Board—An independent agency created by the National Labor Relations Act of 1935 (Wagner Act), as amended by the acts of 1947 (Taft-Hartley Act) and 1959 (Landrum-Griffin Act), established to regulate the relations between employers and employees.

National Mediation Board—Organization created by Congress in 1934, amending the Railway Labor Act, for the purpose of mediating disputes over wages, hours and working conditions that arise between rail and air carriers, and their employees.

Negotiated Settlement—Refers to charges that are settled with benefits to the charging party as warranted by evidence of record. In such cases, the EEOC is a party to the settlement agreement between the charging party and the respondent, who may be an employer, union, or other entity covered by EEOC-enforced statutes.

No Reasonable Cause—Refers to the EEOC's determination that there is "no reasonable cause" to believe that discrimination occurred based upon the evidence obtained in investigation. The charging party may request a review of a no-cause finding by EEOC Headquarters officials and may exercise the right to bring private court action.

Quid Pro Quo Harassment—Latin for "something for something." Quid pro quo harassment is a form of sexual harassment where a manager, supervisor or a person of authority gives or withholds a work-related benefit in exchange for sexual favors. Typically, the harasser requires sexual favors from the victim, either rewarding or punishing the victim in some way.

Reasonable Cause—Refers to the EEOC's determination of "reasonable cause" to believe that discrimination occurred based upon evidence obtained in investigation. Reasonable cause determinations are generally followed by efforts to conciliate the discriminatory issues that gave rise to the initial charge. Some reasonable cause findings are resolved through negotiated settlements, withdrawals with benefits, and other types of resolutions, which are not characterized as either successful or unsuccessful conciliations.

Reinstatement—Refers to the return of an employee to employment from which he or she was illegally dismissed.

Remedy—Refers to the means by which a right is enforced or a violation of a right is compensated.

Retaliation—Overt or covert acts of reprisal against an individual who makes a discrimination complaint, or who cooperates with a discrimination investigation or proceeding.

Salary—Monetary compensation paid by an employer to an employee for job performance.

Scope of Employment—Those activities performed while carrying out the business of one's employer.

Severance Pay—Monies paid to a terminated employee.

Sexual Harassment—Any unwelcome sexual advance, request for sexual favors, or verbal, written or physical conduct of a sexual nature by a manager, supervisor or co-worker.

Shift—Refers to an employee's regular work hours.

Shift Differential—Premium pay earned by an employee who works an unusual or inconvenient shift, e.g. night shift.

Straight Time Pay—Wages paid to an employee for working his or her regular hours.

Strike—A concerted stoppage of work by employees.

Successful Conciliation—Refers to a charge with reasonable cause determination that is closed after successful conciliation. Successful conciliation results in substantial relief to the charging party and all others adversely affected by the discrimination.

Sweat Shop—A business that employs workers under poor working conditions at extremely low wages.

Take-Home Pay—Net wages paid to an employee after all applicable deductions are subtracted.

Temporary Employee—An employee who is hired to work on a short-term basis.

Termination—Refers to cessation of employment, e.g. by quitting or dismissal.

Title VII—Refers to Title VII of the Civil Rights Act of 1964 that prohibits discrimination in employment based on race, color, religion, sex or national origin.

Union Shop—A workplace where all of the employees are members of a union.

Unsuccessful Conciliation—Refers to a charge with reasonable cause determination that is closed after efforts to conciliate the charge are unsuccessful. Pursuant to Commission policy, the field office will close the charge and review it for litigation consideration. Because "reasonable cause" has been found, an unsuccessful conciliation is considered a merit resolution.

Wages—Compensation paid to an employee.

Whistleblower—An employee who reports on violations of the law that occur in the workplace.

White Collar Workers—Generally refers to individuals engaged in office work.

Withdrawal with Benefits—Refers to a charge that is withdrawn by the charging party upon receipt of the desired benefits. The withdrawal may take place after a settlement or after the respondent grants the appropriate benefit to the charging party.

Workplace Harassment—Any unwelcome verbal, written or physical conduct that either denigrates or shows hostility or aversion towards a person on the basis of race, color, national origin, age, sex, religion, disability, marital status or pregnancy that: (1) has the purpose or effect of creating an intimidating, hostile or offensive work environment; (2) has the purpose or effect of unreasonably interfering with an employee's work performance; or (3) affects an employee's employment opportunities or compensation.

Wrongful Discharge—An unlawful dismissal of an employee.

BIBLIOGRAPHY

The American Civil Liberties Union. (Date Visited: September 2007) http://www.aclu.org.

Black's Law Dictionary, Fifth Edition. St. Paul, MN: West Publishing Company, 1979.

Cornell Law School Legal Information Institute. (Date Visited: September 2007) http://www.law.cornell.edu/.

The First Amendment Center. (Date Visited: September 2007) http://www.freedomforum.org/first/welcome.asp/.

The Office of Special Counsel for Immigration Related Unfair Employment Practices. (Date Visited: September 2007) http://www.usdoj.gov/crt/osc/.

The United States Department of Justice. (Date Visited: September 2007) http://www.usdoj.gov/.

The United States Department of Labor. (Date Visited: September 2007) http://www.dol.gov/.

The United States Equal Employment Opportunity Commission. (Date Visited: September 2007) http://www.eeoc.gov/.